W9-AVI-148

HOT-BUTTON ISSUES FOR TEACHERS

What Every Educator Needs to Know about Leadership, Testing, Textbooks, Vouchers, and More

Philip D. Vairo
Sheldon Marcus
Max Weiner

Rowman & Littlefield Education
Lanham, Maryland • Toronto • Plymouth, UK
2007

Published in the United States of America
by Rowman & Littlefield Education
A Division of Rowman & Littlefield Publishers, Inc.
A wholly owned subsidiary of The Rowman & Littlefield Publishing Group, Inc.
4501 Forbes Boulevard, Suite 200, Lanham, Maryland 20706
www.rowmaneducation.com

Estover Road
Plymouth PL6 7PY
United Kingdom

Copyright © 2007 by Philip D. Vairo, Sheldon Marcus, and Max Weiner

All rights reserved. No part of this publication may be reproduced,
stored in a retrieval system, or transmitted in any form or by any
means, electronic, mechanical, photocopying, recording, or otherwise,
without the prior permission of the publisher.

British Library Cataloguing in Publication Information Available

Library of Congress Cataloging-in-Publication Data
Vairo, Philip D.
  Hot-button issues for teachers : what every educator needs to know about
leadership, testing, textbooks, vouchers, and more / Philip D. Vairo, Sheldon
Marcus, Max Weiner.
     p. cm.
  Includes bibliographical references and index.
  ISBN-13: 978-1-57886-626-7 (hardcover : alk. paper)
  ISBN-10: 1-57886-626-X (hardcover : alk. paper)
  ISBN-13: 978-1-57886-627-4 (pbk. : alk. paper)
  ISBN-10: 1-57886-627-8 (pbk. : alk. paper)
  1. Teachers–United States. 2. Effective teaching–United States. I. Marcus,
Sheldon. II. Weiner, Max. III. Title.
  LB1775.2.V35 2007
  371.1–dc22   2007007567

∞™ The paper used in this publication meets the minimum requirements of
American National Standard for Information Sciences—Permanence of
Paper for Printed Library Materials, ANSI/NISO Z39.48-1992.
Manufactured in the United States of America.

This book is dedicated to our colleagues
in the teaching profession.

CONTENTS

ACKNOWLEDGMENTS

No book can be written solely by the individuals whose names appear on the cover, and this book is not an exception. We have had the good fortune to be assisted in our efforts by a number of individuals, and included among them are Pamela Barone and Mina Lev-Drewes. They have been invaluable to us through their reliability, word-processing skills, and editorial comments. They also kept us on task and were most patient and efficient in their calmness as we constantly rewrote our manuscript.

We owe a debt to our wives, Lillian, Phyllis, and Gloria, for their patience, understanding, and support while we worked on this manuscript.

A special thank you to Bonnie Heatzig for helping in the preparation of the preliminary proposal submitted to our publisher, Rowman & Littlefield. We thank Dr. Thomas F. Koerner, vice president at Rowman & Littlefield, and Paul Cacciato, associate editor, for their confidence and support. Special thanks are also extended to Andrew Yoder of Rowman & Littlefield.

PREFACE:
WHO WROTE THIS BOOK AND WHY?

The undertaking of this book has special meaning to the authors. In total, we have been teachers at all levels of education for well over 150 years. In this volume, we have attempted to identify and discuss the basic issues facing the teaching profession today.

The motivating force for writing this book is the authors' hope to alert those in the profession and the American public that decisive steps need to be initiated to address the nation's educational problems and to provide practical advice to address these problems. It is our intention to present the reader with numerous issues that are in the forefront of the heated debate about the teaching profession. The mounting interest and public concerns about the schoolhouse and the teaching profession give special timeliness to this task.

Last year, Marcus and Vairo coauthored *Hot-Button Issues in Today's Schools: What Every Parent Needs to Know*, published by Rowman & Littlefield. That book was the first in a series of books that the authors planned to write. We thought it would be only natural that this second book in the series would focus on the teaching profession. Obviously, both books touch on some common ground and subjects about which both parents and teachers have a vital stake.

In this book, the authors have attempted to cover the broad educational spectrum of pressing problems facing teachers. The topics included in this book include a variety of subjects ranging from violence in our schools, salaries, merit pay, teacher accountability, testing, national standards, ethics, teacher burnout, pedagogy vs. subject matter content, and a host of other related and pertinent topics that are of special interest to teachers, administrators, parents, political leaders, and the general public.

The rationale for giving our readers a brief biographical history of the authors is to provide an insight into our background and experiences, in order that they may better appreciate who we are and thus have a greater understanding of the perspectives we present. Since this book is predicated on our research, experiences, and observations as teachers at all levels of education, from the lower grades through doctoral programs in education, it is essential that we provide you with information about us.

All three authors are sons of poor, limited-English-speaking immigrant parents who had a firm belief in America and all its hopes and dreams. Our parents recognized early in their arrival to this new land that the answer to fulfilling their dreams for their children was through education. Therefore, it is not surprising that all three of us became teachers. Throughout our careers we have been committed to providing our students with the best education that we were capable of delivering to them in spite of the problems that our profession has faced over the decades. The authors' biographical statements follow.

Dr. Philip D. Vairo received his doctorate from Duke University. He has held teaching and administrative positions covering the education gamut—from classroom teacher, school counselor, college professor, dean, academic vice president, and president. He has been affiliated with the New York City public school system, Hunter College, the University of North Carolina, the University of Tennessee, California State University at Los Angeles, Palm Beach Atlantic University, Touro College, Fordham University, and Worcester State College, where he served as president.

Dr. Vairo has coauthored five books: *Urban Education: Problems and Prospect*; *How to Teach Disadvantaged Youth*; *Learning and Teaching in the Elementary School*; *Urban Education: Opportunity or Crisis?*; and *Hot-Button Issues in Today's School: What Every Parent Needs to*

Know. Additionally, he has authored numerous monographs and chapters in texts and over 60 articles in professional journals.

Dr. Sheldon Marcus is the author of *Father Coughlin: The Tumultuous Life of the Priest of the Little Flower*; he is also the coauthor of *Conflicts in Urban Education*; *Urban Education: Crisis or Opportunity?*; *Administrative Decision Making in Schools: A Case Study Approach to Strategic Planning*; and *Hot-Button Issues in Today's Schools: What Every Parent Needs to Know*. Dr. Marcus has also authored or coauthored over 100 articles, monographs, grants, evaluations, and reviews. His work has appeared in such publications as the *Journal of American History*, the *Teachers College Record*, the *Peabody Journal of Education*, *America Magazine*, and the *Journal of Teacher Education*.

Dr. Marcus has made numerous speeches to professional organizations and has served on many panels and workshops with a host of nationally renowned educators.

Dr. Max Weiner is a former public school science teacher and school counselor. After receiving his doctorate from Yale University, he taught at Brooklyn College and the City University of New York Graduate Center. Eventually, he also served as associate dean, university dean of teacher education, and professor of education there. For 12 years, Dr. Weiner was dean of the Graduate School of Education at Fordham University, where he is presently dean emeritus. He was also affiliated with Touro College.

Dr. Weiner is the author of over 100 scholarly publications, research papers, and grants. Dr. Weiner has served on advisory boards, on accreditation evaluation teams, and as a consultant to school districts throughout the country.

I

THE TEACHING PROFESSION TODAY

❶

THE STATUS OF THE TEACHING PROFESSION: WHERE ARE WE GOING?

There is no disguising the fact that the teaching profession is faced with complex problems. Historically, this has always been the case. Since Horace Mann's day in the early to mid-19th century, American education has been faced with complex problems. Today is no different. The bottom line was and remains the same: what content should be taught, by whom should this content be taught, and how can it be best taught so that students can absorb the material. Easy solutions to elevate the status of the profession are frequently proposed but few have been truly effective. Of course, there are solutions—or, more realistically, partial solutions—to deal with the issues raised in this chapter, but implementing any remedies will be predicated on the outcome of continuous, fierce battles among the executive branch, the U.S. Congress, state legislatures, state departments of education, the National Education Association (NEA), the American Federation of Teachers (AFT), lobbyists, taxpayer groups, and the courts.

There is no concerted effort nationwide to raise the status of the teaching profession. There are some feeble attempts that are piecemeal efforts, but there is no comprehensive distinctive dialogue addressing the status of the profession. Simply said, a vision for the future of the teaching profession needs to be developed.

American society is stratified along such factors as income, inherited wealth, family ties, educational attainment, and occupation. Additionally, status in our society is also dependent on age, race, ethnic, background, religious affiliation, gender, citizenship, and sexual orientation. Furthermore, social institutions within our society have stratification and status imbedded in their organizational framework. For example, the Catholic Church has deacons, sisters, brothers, priests, auxiliary bishops, bishops, cardinals, and the pope as functionaries, all of whom have specific duties and an assigned status in the hierarchal structure of the church. Professional baseball has developed a tier structure that carries special status. For example, playing in the major leagues is more respected than playing in the minor leagues. The military, of course, has developed a rank structure that reflects power, status, and prestige.

The classification of people and groups in the social order is indeed a common but complex process and often defies logical explanations. Teaching, although not usually thought to be among the premier status professions in many opinion polls, has played a crucial role in promoting social and economic mobility in our society and providing the intellectual, vocational, and social skills to enable millions of Americans to fulfill the "American Dream." Nevertheless, with perhaps the exception of the period of the Great Depression from 1929–1941, when entry into the profession was highly competitive and few but the rich and the academically talented went to college, teachers in grades K–12 have never been perceived as conveyors of scholarly knowledge, as have university professors. Teaching in grades K–12 has been viewed in an entirely different perspective, usually as focusing on rudimentary basic learning tasks.

Society's values and perceived images of teachers are reflected in the modest status in which the teaching profession is regarded. The place of the teaching profession in the "pecking order" can change, but it is a slow process that entails mass public education, professional reforms, the raising of entry and retention standards, and the recruitment of outstanding people to the profession.

There is debate among sociologists and professionals in various fields over the prerequisites for membership in a profession. The definition of the term "professional" is as complex as the specific criteria one would use to classify an occupation as a profession. Historically, theology, law, and medicine have been accepted as the premier status professions, and we believe they still maintain this status today. Currently, the label of "professional" is also accorded to accountants, dentists, engineers, and to those in high-tech fields. Teachers still hold marginal status as "professionals" because many in the general public do not believe teachers meet some of the basic criteria that would qualify them as "professionals." Yes, a bachelor's degree is required of teachers and a master's degree is recommended, as they are for most members of other professions. On the other hand, admission standards to the teaching profession are not as rigorous as they should be. Teacher preparation programs often do not attract highly qualified students. The affiliation of teachers with unions is viewed with suspicion by many and gives teaching a "labor union" label. The profession lacks autonomy because of its civil service status.

Today, teachers are involved in providing many services in which they were not professionally prepared and that go far beyond instructional responsibilities. Although the authors believe teaching merits "professional" status, throughout this book we make proposals to upgrade the profession. The authors have no doubt that if our proposed changes are incorporated into professional practices, teaching will qualify as a "real profession" in the 21st century. On the other hand, the authors believe that if the teaching establishment continues with its present practices, then the public will view teaching as simply a glorified civil service position with a guaranteed life appointment, a good pension, and excellent medical coverage.

It is interesting to note that until the 1960s, high school teachers were paid more than elementary or junior high school teachers. This practice has been remedied over the past several decades, and now teachers are paid by degrees held, seniority, and in a few cases, through merit recognition. This has been a step in the right direction. But regardless of this effort, the present state of affairs in the teaching profession is unsatisfactory. Many schools are staffed by poorly prepared teachers with minimal qualifications, and some are teaching out of license or without certification.

It was reported in the *Christian Science Monitor* (March 8, 2005) in a research study conducted by Caroline Horby and Andrew Leigh that low salaries is the primary reason talented women are not drawn to the teaching profession. On July 15, 2003, the same newspaper reported that males shy away from the teaching profession primarily because of low salaries, poor status, and negative stereotypes associated with teaching. Les Krantz, in the *Jobs Rated Almanac* published in 2002, ranked careers by a composite of six core job criteria, which included income, stress, physical demands, perks, job satisfaction, and outlook. Teaching was ranked 125th out of 250 careers. In 2006, teaching was not included as one of the excellent careers cited on the *U.S. News and World Report* website.

Ronald A. Reis, in *The Everything Hot Careers Book*, investigated careers that he classified "hot careers" and "hot choices." To our disappointment, teaching was not mentioned—but we were not really surprised. Teaching in our estimation is an exciting profession but its status and image do not always measure up to other "hot" career choices that, in reality, may not be as "hot" or exciting as teaching.

It is encouraging today that some states are making efforts to address such issues as supply and demand and teacher salaries. The *News and Observer* on May 23, 2006, stated that North Carolina was planning to pay teachers depending on what subjects they teach and where they teach. Florida Governor Jeb Bush, on January 23, 2006, as reported in the *Orlando Sentinel*, indicated he wants to provide all teachers with a laptop computer and help defray college costs for teachers who are recruited from out of state.

New York City is now offering licensed mathematics, science, and special education high school teachers with housing incentives worth up to $15,000 to teach in New York City. The selected teachers will teach in schools faced with critical shortages in these areas. Advertisements are appearing in such newspapers as the *New York Times* promoting this program, and recruiters are seeking applicants from across the nation. How successful those efforts will be remains to be seen.

The Palm Beach County School District in Florida has initiated an incentive plan for teachers who agree to teach in one of six "D" or "F" low-performing schools involved in a pilot program. Teachers would be required to agree to extend their school day by one hour and teach 10 extra school days. A 20% salary bonus plus other pay incentives would be available to those who sign on.

In spite of these cited efforts, the teaching profession continues to be faced with a degree of snobbery directed at K–6 teachers by those who teach in high school. Such snobbery pales in comparison to the views of faculty at colleges and universities toward K–12 teachers, particularly among faculty not in schools of education. Of course, it is also some-times true that many higher education faculty look down at colleagues in departments or schools of education in their own institutions. Within each of these structural levels, further differentiation exists, whether one teaches at one of the "best" universities, colleges, or private institu-tions or at a less prestigious school.

Every year *U.S. News and World Report* ranks America's best col-leges. There is a strong status symbol associated with where a school is ranked. For example, Harvard, Princeton, Yale, University of Pennsyl-vania, Duke, M.I.T., Stanford, and California Institute of Technology all usually receive top ratings as national universities. Also included in this annual issue are the top 50 public national universities, the top univer-sities offering master's degrees, and the top comprehensive colleges at the bachelor's level. In addition, liberal arts colleges are also included in this survey. This report conveys to the general public, as well as to the college faculty employed at those institutions, that a very hierarchical, stratified tier structure exists in American higher education.

In May 2006, *Newsweek* ranked 1,200 top U.S. public high schools. Included on this list were: (1) Talented and Gifted (Dallas); (2) Jeffer-son County IBS (Alabama); (3) Basis Charter (Tucson); (4) City Honors (Buffalo); (5) Stanton College Prep (Jacksonville); and (6) Eastside (Gainesville), just to name a selected few. Here again, status and pres-tige are introduced. One can readily contest the criteria used in both the *U.S. News and World Report* and *Newsweek* studies. Nevertheless, these studies reinforce the authors' thesis that stratification and status exist at all levels of the teaching profession.

Frank Leana's book *The Best Private Schools and How to Get In* fur-ther illustrates that the educational establishment is highly stratified. Teachers and students at such elite private schools such as Dalton, Cheshire, Loomis, Horace Mann, and Chapin are at the top echelon of the private school establishment.

The following benchmarks play a significant role in the teacher's pro-fessional identity and status:

- The grade level at which one teaches
- The prestige and status of the university, college, or school where one teaches

- The subject that one teaches
- The advanced degrees that one holds
- The institutions from which one received his or her degrees

When teachers in grades K–12 are compared with other profession-als, such as doctors, scientists, engineers, and college professors, along with individuals who have majored in such disciplines as mathematics, biology, chemistry, physics, finance, and engineering, they usually do not command comparable salaries and professional respect. It is worth not-ing that the NEA, at its 2006 national meeting, called for a minimum starting salary of $40,000 a year for teachers. This is a very modest re-quest and far below the starting salaries for jobs in the occupations listed above. It should also be noted that some school districts around the country already offer $40,000+ salaries to starting teachers with a bach-elor's degree. Sadly, many other school districts do not yet approach such a starting salary.

There are many reasons why teaching has had serious difficulties rep-resenting itself as a profession. Listed below are many of the problems and suggested remedies proposed by the authors that would reflect fa-vorably on the teaching profession.

- A competitive salary schedule must be established. The authors have found that almost half of all teachers seek additional employ-ment because their salaries are inadequate to support their fami-lies. Our society needs educators who can afford to devote their full-time energies to teaching.
- Many teachers cannot afford to live in the districts where they teach. For example, the states of California and Florida are facing an affordable housing crisis because of the real estate housing boom in affluent areas of those states. This critical shortage has af-fected teachers' ability to live and teach in many such communities. We cannot afford to alienate and lose the services of teachers be-cause of the lack of affordable housing.
- The master's degree must be the minimal requirement to enter the teaching profession. Only 60 percent of teachers presently hold a master's degree, and very few K–12 teachers possess a doctorate. It

is important that these advanced degrees have a significant relationship to the subject taught by a teacher.

- Somewhere between 10 and 15% of all teachers hold temporary and substitute licenses. Many are teaching out of their subject license, and in areas in which they have minimal academic preparation. This is especially true in mathematics and the sciences. In the premier professions, the functionary must be fully qualified to perform the duties of the position.
- Teachers have extended vacation periods, numerous holidays, and conference and workshop days. The workday is usually shorter than many other professions. The school year should be extended from the present 180 days, which is usually followed by most districts, to 210–220 days, which would be similar to what is required in such countries as China, Japan, South Korea, and India. Why not give our students maximum exposure to learning?
- It is not surprising that some people in the general population do not have favorable memories of their own educational experiences or their teachers. A concerted effort must be made to change their impressions by combining academic rigor with teachers who truly care for their students.
- Teachers who gain tenure usually have lifetime positions regardless of their performance. This does not pass muster with the general public. The general public looks upon tenure with suspicion and as a vehicle to protect incompetent teachers. Very few tenured teachers are terminated from their positions, and the process of revoking tenure is too cumbersome and time consuming. The process must be streamlined so that administrators do not face insurmountable time and expense barriers if they try to revoke a teacher's tenure due to poor performance. This must be done while the due process rights of teachers are ensured, so that they may be safe from dictatorial, autocratic, and/or incompetent administrators.
- Schools of education usually have low status in the informal university pecking order. Schools such as medicine, law, arts and sciences, and engineering have far greater academic respectability than schools of education.
- Universities and colleges seldom commit adequate resources to schools of education.

- Teacher education programs in our universities and colleges lack academic credibility in the eyes of colleagues in other disciplines and, at times, even with those students who are involved in teacher education programs.
- A merit pay system must supplement the present lock-step salary increments.
- The placement of huge numbers of inexperienced teachers and the retention of experienced but mediocre ones in schools in low socioeconomic areas are obviously not appropriate. There is a need to decide what initial experience is best for the teacher. More experienced but still energetic teachers, rather than neophytes, should be placed in the more difficult schools.
- Accountability must be translated into action in every classroom. Teachers, like all workers in our society, cannot be sheltered from periodic classroom performance evaluations.
- Substitute, temporary, emergency, and all substandard teaching licenses should be abolished. Albert Shanker used to ask, "Would you place yourself under the care of a provisionally certified or temporary doctor?" The answer is obvious.
- Within schools of education, the statuses of the respective departments are ranked informally by faculty and students. Usually, the department preparing teachers usually has the lowest status. Faculty in the departments of educational leadership, counseling, and school psychology, in particular, often see themselves as being more research and scientifically oriented than their colleagues in teacher preparation programs.
- There is a need to upgrade admission, graduation, and classroom standards in the teacher preparation programs at both the undergraduate and graduate levels in all areas.
- To complicate matters further, the educational community in grades K–12 has developed an internal status ladder within its own organization that gives greater recognition, remuneration, and status to school counselors, deans, assistant principals, principals, and other nonclassroom personnel. In essence, the classroom teacher is at the bottom of the educational pay scale. It seems that we have forgotten that teachers are the key instructional individuals in the

school. Salaries for competent teachers should not be below those of nonteaching educational professionals.

- Our competitive position in the world depends on an educated citizenry and qualified and well-prepared teachers. There needs to be an effective, meaningful partnership between educators in grades K–12 and professors. This can be best accomplished through quality, field-based programs between school districts and teacher preparation programs.

- There is a need to recruit outstanding students to careers in education through scholarships, special financial packages, and fellowships.

- Many professors preparing teachers have often not taught in grades K–12 for many years, if at all. Many do not even spend meaningful amounts of time in K–12 schools, if any time at all. Professors need to return to the K–12 environment and obtain firsthand experiences for at least one semester every seven years. It is interesting to note that William Perel and Philip D. Vairo, in an article that was published in *Educational Forum* almost four decades ago, wrote about this issue and made a similar proposal, but it has never been adopted by any school of education as a basic requirement. We are forced to conclude that most professors do not *want* to return to the K–12 environment!

- Unfortunately, perhaps the most important sequence in the teacher education training program—student teaching—is in desperate need of repair. The time and energy devoted to working with student teachers is usually assigned to the untenured college faculty members or nontenure-track clinical staff. Student teaching, in essence, is a short duration experience, oftentimes just one semester, with inadequate college supervision. Cooperating teachers are not provided with adequate remuneration, training, and incentives to serve as cooperating teachers. They usually receive no reduction in load or compensation other than a free course at the college sponsoring the student teacher.

- Old ways are difficult to change. A nationwide competitive salary scale for teachers must be instituted, with partial support from the federal government. Of course, regional costs of living must be considered in the equation. However, the inequitable system of supporting education that relies heavily on local taxes cannot be continued. Wealthy communities do indeed monopolize the job market by attracting the best qualified teachers to their districts because of their strong financial base.

- As long as the number of high school dropouts increases and many K–12 students fail to perform up to grade level, the status of the profession is in jeopardy. Employers contend that many high school graduates who enter the job market essentially are functionally illiterate. The first step in changing the public's perception of the teaching profession is to be successful in the academic preparation of our K–12 students.

The *New York Times* reported on May 24, 2006, that the United States is facing a critical nursing shortage and that there is some discussion to recruit more nurses from abroad. In this same edition, the *New York Times* reported that a business executive was receiving millions in his salary and benefits package, and had received continuous salary increases at the same time the value of company stock was dropping because of poor earnings. This story is not unique in the business world.

There appears to be a need to reexamine and scrutinize the basic ways in which we give recognition and status to the various professional positions in our society. The fabric of American life and its core values are being threatened by our unwillingness to alter our hierarchal status structure. If capitalism and American democracy are going to survive, it is imperative that professions like nursing and teaching are elevated in the pecking order of our social structure.

One of the authors recalls a story told to him by an elderly retired surgeon who practiced in New York City. He remembered that there was a time when teaching was the envy and the preferred choice of the top students graduating from New York City public high schools. Teachers were offered comparatively good salaries, and the professional status of teaching was recognized with respect. The surgeon recalled that although he was an outstanding student in biology and passed the rigid New York City examination, there were many students who scored higher than he did, and he was not selected for a teaching position. Jobs were scarce during the Great Depression, but teaching was one of the premier career choices. Denied the opportunity to become a teacher, he applied to medical school and was admitted.

The authors hope that the day will once again arrive where the most talented students decide to select teaching as their career preference. Why not? The teaching climate in the United States can improve to a degree where, once again, teaching can be included among the most sought-after careers by our brightest students. This can be accomplished if the general public feels the need to exercise its desire through the ballot to make teaching a highly valued profession. Whether this will happen may depend on how the issue is framed and presented to the public by the parties involved in education, some of whom have a vested interest in maintaining the status quo.

In the final analysis, if the problems facing American schools are to be solved, it will be through well-qualified, capable, understanding teachers who possess confidence and self-esteem and who receive competitive professional salaries. Although there are no sure panaceas, now is the time to act!

KEY QUESTIONS FOR TEACHERS

1. How do you view teaching as a career?
2. Do you believe teaching is a profession?
3. What level of academic preparation should be required of teachers?
4. Should teachers be able to hold an after-school or summer job?
5. Are you looking for a position outside of teaching in another school district?
6. Do you live in the district in which you teach?
7. Can you afford to live in the district in which you teach?
8. Do you support the idea that better qualified teachers would enter the profession if salaries were higher?
9. Should teacher salaries reflect the laws of supply and demand of teachers in the academic marketplace?
10. Should we allow individuals who do not meet all the requirements for certification to teach?

2

DECISION MAKERS WHO INFLUENCE EDUCATIONAL POLICY: WHO ARE THEY?

All social institutions in our society include decision makers. In education, these important functionaries may be inside the professional educational establishment or be external parties who have vested and/or professional interests, legal obligations, and legislative responsibilities in attaining specific goals and objectives. There is no doubt that the educational establishment has a host of decision makers converging on its door with recommendations and policy issues.

Because all the educational constituent groups believe they have first-hand knowledge and understanding of the problems associated with teaching, they are likely to be more active participants in the decision-making process as opposed to, for example, patients who may be more reluctant to join the debate about hospital medical procedures or budgetary matters because of their total lack of knowledge of those subjects.

There is no doubt that the bosses and stakeholders in the decision-making process have changed over the decades. Behind every decision, there are sometimes just a few leaders behind the scenes or, in other circumstances, there are many individuals, professional associations, and groups of interested citizens who play an important role in the public policy issues related to education. What is of particular interest is that the alignment of individuals and groups change from issue to issue.

There is another group of people who are frequently called the "outsiders" or "inactive players." These citizens usually do not participate in everyday school policies but only become active when an issue on which they have strong views—such as sex education, evolution, or textbook content—surfaces in the public arena.

So who are the constituents who are the active players in formulating new policies, defending and/or opposing the status quo, searching for new ideas, and encouraging experimentation and research to obtain answers to the pressing educational problems facing our schools?

On one hand, the authors welcome any debate about education that is in the public forum of ideas, with almost every advocacy group conceivable in our society participating in this dialogue. Education is probably the only social institution where so large a segment of the American population is not reluctant to share views and join the debate about what is wrong with our schools. To the authors' regret, however, teachers in most states still have a limited voice in the shaping of the broad policies that have an impact on the profession. It is practically impossible to cite all the groups that play a role in formulating policy and/or influencing the decisions in education. The authors nevertheless attempt to chronicle these groups in broad categories to show the reader the complex maze of public and private bodies interacting on the educational scene. These groups include the following:

- Politicians in our federal, state, and local governments
- Judges who administer our courts and rule on school litigation matters
- Local boards of education, the U.S. Department of Education, and the state departments of education
- Teachers' associations such as the National Education Association (NEA) and the American Federation of Teachers (AFT)
- Parent groups such as National Parent Association
- Taxpayer associations
- Minority, religious, gay rights, and gender groups
- Political and legal action groups, such as the American Civil Liberties Union
- Subject-centered professional associations representing English, social studies, mathematics, and science teachers, just to name a few

- School administrators, counselors, psychologists, and social workers
- Private foundations, such as the Gates Foundation and the Ford Foundation
- Public educational networks
- Various media figures, such as Hollywood actors, newspaper journalists, radio talk show hosts, public and private television producers, and newspaper editorial boards
- Many, many other constituents, stakeholders, and advocacy groups who have an impact on school policy

It is quite obvious that obtaining some consensus in education has always been a challenging task. From the very beginning, the American educational scene has witnessed sharp disagreements relative to practically every issue facing the teaching profession. The relative weight of the respective decision makers and those who influence policy in the educational process has changed from time to time in our history.

For example, the federal government, the courts, civil rights groups, organizations such as the American Civil Liberties Union, and the Heritage Foundation are playing larger roles in the decision-making process today than ever before, while local boards of education, state departments of education, and even school superintendents and principals have been somewhat marginalized in the new power struggle evolving on the education scene.

Teachers, however, have never been a domineering force in determining school policies, even though the NEA and the AFT have gained considerable influence in the past 40 years. Our nation needs to recognize that an important resource, our K–12 teachers, must become partners in the decision-making process of what happens in our schools and how teachers are prepared.

In some respects, the authors have admiration for the efforts of the NEA and the AFT. But when these organizations attempt to introduce factory-like labor regulations and, because of self-interest, oppose the extended school year and day, and use teacher union dues to support specific political candidates, they hurt the status of the teaching profession. Often one finds teacher unions defending teachers who have violated the public trust, teachers who should be terminated, and teachers who use the classrooms for political, economic, and social activism.

These actions weaken the teachers' image in the forum of public opinion and stereotype their professional organizations and status. The image of teacher unions has been further eroded by fiscal corruption within a number of local affiliates.

Let us be clear. Regardless of the shortcomings of teacher unions and the positions that they sometimes take, professionally, teachers must play a primary role in educational matters. Teachers are in the frontlines of the learning and teaching process. Their voices need not only to be heard but also to be taken seriously by decision makers.

The one battle that teachers must win is to upgrade the certification requirements for entry into the teaching profession. Although many influential pressure groups readily agree with the premise that America needs outstanding teachers, the problem is that there are many different perspectives on how to specifically accomplish this task.

Many years ago, when one of the authors was an undergraduate enrolled in a basic economics course, the professor discussed the many forces at work that have an impact on our economic system. He pointed out that, regardless of the influence of the key decision makers in our society, supply and demand ruled the marketplace. Therefore, if any group of workers is in short supply, and the demand is great for their services, it is inevitable that those workers' wages will increase. However, as long as there are forces at work that support temporary, substitute, or out-of-license employment of teachers in the schoolhouse, teacher salaries will be deflated because the supply is being met.

Only when there is a pressing need for essential services and no one to provide them will things happen. Teacher groups must apply this age-old economic principle to the issues at hand. Let us focus on the basic rule of competitive capitalism. If the profession controls supply when the demand warrants additional teachers, we shall see a breakthrough despite the power brokers and influence peddlers.

The history of corporate/industrial relations with unions has had both positive and negative levels of difficulties. This has also been true with the complex relationships among teachers, the decision makers, and those who influence the decision makers. There are many avenues open to teachers to influence and determine educational policies. No stone should be left uncovered in the profession's quest to have a voice. When it comes to educational policies, teachers can no longer sit on the sidelines and let other groups make the vital decisions. Teachers need to become partners in the decision-making process and just have the power to veto or subvert positive educational change.

KEY QUESTIONS FOR TEACHERS

1. Who do you believe are the decision makers in education?
2. Do you have a voice in the decision-making process in your school or district?
3. What teacher groups do you perceive to hold the most power in the decision-making process?
4. Are you satisfied with the decisions that are made in education? If not, why?
5. Do you ask politicians about where they stand on educational issues?
6. What is your opinion of your state department of education? Are you satisfied with its performance?
7. Do you think broad-based participation in the decision-making process would improve the quality of education?
8. Have you ever been a decision maker in any social institution? What was your reaction to the experience?
9. Do you believe the average teacher will ever have a real voice in decision making?
10. What recommendations would you propose to improve the decision-making process in education?

3

COMPETITION IN THE EDUCATIONAL SCENE TODAY: IS THIS A NEW ERA?

This chapter focuses on competing educational enterprises, such as homeschool instruction, charter schools, voucher systems, online instruction, profit-making schools, bogus schools, and private and religious schools.

Competition in the educational establishment has been intensifying during the past decade. After years of a virtual monopoly by traditional educational thinkers, an intense and bitter battle has surfaced with the introduction of new approaches to learning. Today, there are definite changes taking place in the ways people are receiving their education.

There are ripples of trepidation and concern within the ranks of the teaching profession about these competing educational enterprises. These concerns are both expressions of self-serving interests as well as legitimate academic questions.

One of the most attractive institutions surfacing on the American educational scene is homeschooling. Although it is difficult to quantify the number of students who receive homeschooling, it is estimated that from one to three million students are being educated in their homes. Most homeschooling is usually undertaken by one or both parents but, increasingly, private profit-making businesses have entered the homeschool market.

Homeschooling is a legal educational alternative. Those who are involved in teaching homeschooling do not need to obtain a state teaching certificate. It is, in essence, a one-to-one or small group tutorial approach that has embraced the basic principles of individualized instruction; time flexibility according to academic needs; learning in a safe, caring environment; and the freedom to select subjects like religious instruction and spiritual values and to shape the teaching of such controversial subjects as sex education, drug use, evolution, race, and abortion.

Obviously, educators are concerned that parents may not possess the educational training and resources to appropriately educate their children. Children in homeschool settings have limited opportunities for social interaction with other children. However, homeschooled students appear to be succeeding academically and are developing reputations for being self-directed learners.

The competition between homeschool instruction and traditional education is now focusing on whether school districts have special obligations to the homeschooled learner. For example, do school districts have to make available to the homeschooled student extracurricular activities after school and specialized enrichment activities and courses such as art, computers, music, and physical education? What about the use of textbooks, curriculum guides, and attending advanced college placement classes? Many school districts are resisting the notion of providing many of these support services. Are homeschooled students eligible for participation in athletic teams and school sports? This list is never ending. Many of these issues are currently in litigation before various courts. In the meantime, a number of state legislatures have already passed some laws guaranteeing homeschooled students access to school activities.

The authors have serious reservations about homeschooling. However, if the homeschooled student has access to many of the services available to all the taxpaying constituents, we are more inclined to give this approach a chance. However, the jury is still out on the issues associated with homeschooling. We are particularly concerned that the private sector is entering the homeschool business. What safeguards will the state establish to protect the participating consumer? Finally, will this new educational entity promote the best interests of the students?

Another competing educational idea that is causing considerable intense controversy is the proposed voucher system. There are different types of voucher systems. Thus, defining vouchers is difficult. In its simplest form, however, think of a voucher as a coupon with a set dollar value, redeemable by parents or children at a school of their choice. Within this definition is the core of the controversy surrounding the voucher system. How much should the voucher be worth? In what kind of school would the vouchers be redeemable? Public schools only? Public schools and sectarian private schools? Would religious-affiliated schools be part of any voucher system? Would this violate the U.S. Constitution by violating the principle of separation of church and state? Would there be geographical limitations on the use of vouchers?

There are those who are afraid that the introduction of a voucher system redeemable at religious and private schools would destroy the public school system. This view is predicated on the view that many parents believe that private secular and religious schools are safer and would offer a better education to their children. Critics of vouchers also claim there would be a real danger of private schools admitting only students who would not present serious academic, emotional, and behavioral problems. The voucher system has supporters and critics from many community constituent groups. The underlying question is whether children in schools where the overall performance level is below expectations and where these schools have failed generations should be given the opportunity to attend private or religious schools. Failing schools are no option for our children.

The question is frequently raised that private and religious-affiliated universities and colleges continue today to receive federal monies directly and indirectly. Furthermore, public, private, and religious higher education institutions in the United States do indeed have the respect of the world academic community. Thousands of foreign students come to our shores to study at public, private, and religious-affiliated institutions of higher education. Our universities and colleges are models of excellence throughout the world. Our great institutions of higher learning are a mixture of private, public, and religious institutions. Universities such as the University of California at Berkeley and Los Angeles, Stanford, Duke, Yale, Harvard, M.I.T., Georgetown, Princeton, Michigan, Texas, and Pennsylvania are just a partial list exemplifying how all three sectors of higher education have prospered. The common bond that these institutions possess should be replicated in our K–12 schools. Our veterans today are receiving economic support, just as their fathers and grandfathers did, to further their education at a school of their choice. Veterans of the World War II era, as well as Korea, Vietnam, and Iraq did not abandon public higher education. All three sectors are stronger today because of the help they and their students received from Uncle Sam.

We are firmly committed to the notion that all of America's children, not just those of the rich, should have a choice of where they can attend school. Obviously, intense controversy exists around the voucher system. Yes, it will bring competition to the public schoolhouse. However, there is competition at our universities, and they all have flourished in the midst of this challenging experience.

As of this date, court decisions are not encouraging, and there is little support in the ranks of the educational establishment to endorse the voucher system. There are many citizens who support a voucher system comparable to the GI Bill of Rights. Public higher education was not hurt by tuition reimbursements to GIs to be used in public as well as private and religious-affiliated universities and colleges. Should not children's rights be the primary consideration in opening the door to all educational institutions that can serve them effectively? Due to opposition from the NEA and the AFT and its supporters in various legislatures, the voucher system today is more of a philosophical idea than a real competing educational threat to our public school system. It is an idea that someday may come of age.

Charter schools are a relatively recent newcomer on the educational scene. This movement began over two decades ago, and now there are about 3,000 schools operating in the United States. The name "charter school" seems to carry a mystic message, giving the impression to the general public that it offers students something very special and qualitatively superior from what is offered in our traditional public schools. In reality, coining a fancy, sophisticated name to promote the illusion of progress and success is misleading.

In theory, charter schools are exempted from much of the paperwork and many of the regulations of a district or state education department for a specified period of time. The time period can range anywhere from 3 to 5 years. At the conclusion of that time period, the charter school must demonstrate that its students are progressing academically and meeting district and state standards. Sadly, due to the federal No Child Left Behind Act (NCLB) requiring states to set and students to meet specific educational standards, we are seeing some states *lowering* educational standards so that they may comply with the NCLB requirements.

The charter school movement may now be a competing educational enterprise, but skeptics like the authors believe it is not necessarily the model for the future. The research that the authors reviewed does not demonstrate that students enrolled in charter schools score higher than those students enrolled in the traditional public schools. In fact, in many instances, charter school students scored lower. Of course, there are those who point out that some charter schools have made academic gains greater than some traditional public schools.

In addition to the academic issues confronting charter schools, the U.S. Department of Education found that many charter schools lack the ability and capacity to adequately oversee their operations. It is also interesting to note that close to 500 charter schools have closed since the movement began. The *New York Times*, in an editorial on May 10, 2006, took the position that charter schools are not a solution to the academic problems facing our schools. The editorial was very clear that the way to improve education was to provide qualified, well-prepared teachers and school environments where learning and teaching can flourish in an orderly setting. The authors concur with this position.

E-learning introduces ways in which the learning does not need to be in the same classroom as the teacher. For decades, correspondence courses and television were utilized when students were unable to attend classes and have direct contact with their teachers. With the advent of the Internet, educational leaders are exploring new learning and teaching models in which distance separates the learner from the teacher. New approaches are now being utilized to enhance the learning and teaching process. These models include the remote classroom model, independent study, and student network interaction. Of course, there are advantages and disadvantages with each model.

The success of the respective model depends on how it is adapted and tailored to meet the educational needs of the learner and the skills of the teacher. The teacher is the key and acts as the resource person and guide. Let us be frank. Regardless of the strategies and technologies, the teacher holds the keys to *any* successful program. The authors see many opportunities for the continued use and introduction of new approaches using the e-learning delivery system. We caution, however, that the user may feel isolated and not sufficiently motivated to independently use this model in his or her learning and teaching process. Nevertheless, e-learning will be with us for a long time, and both students and teachers will need to adapt to this new technology.

Diploma mills and bogus preparatory schools continue to exist throughout the country. These two illegitimate educational enterprises need greater scrutiny and stringent laws carrying stiffer penalties. The states, along with the federal government, should be active participants in monitoring intra- and interstate fraudulent activities.

The National Collegiate Athletic Association (NCAA), after years of relative inaction dealing with the problems associated with bogus preparatory schools attended by athletes, has now begun to be proactive. Because the integrity of college admissions standards is at stake, some universities and colleges are beginning to closely monitor where students complete courses and to review suspect transcripts that are submitted and the accreditation status of the respective school attended. It was reported in the spring of 2006 that athletes were completing courses required for admission at nontraditional schools and enrolling in correspondence courses where they were not required to meet academic standards and in some cases never doing any work to earn the credits that they received. It is encouraging that the NCAA is now attempting to single out the worst offending schools. The screening process should be done by all universities and colleges and include all students who apply for admission. It has also come to the attention of the NCAA that some universities and colleges have special credit courses and independent study programs to assist athletes. These schools have come under scrutiny for their educational practices and loose academic standards. Educational providers at all levels cannot ignore their professional responsibilities to maintain academic standards. To do otherwise will only jeopardize the credibility of American education. Nevertheless, we realize that in some of our colleges and universities, athletic directors and coaches have more power and the support of students, alums, wealthy boosters, and politicians than do the college or university president and faculty. In such cases, if the president wants to keep his or her job, pleading ignorance or denial is the safe course.

Of course, the NCAA has its own income to protect. This income is generated by huge contracts with television networks. So while publicly proclaiming its opposition to academic abuses, the NCAA is careful not to disturb the dollar pipeline it and many of its member institutions enjoy. A few suspensions, some fines—but nothing must be done to seriously interrupt the flow of games into the homes of millions of American households.

There are also many accrediting mills that grant accreditation to schools, but none are recognized by the federal government or by any state, and they carry no weight in the education profession or by bona fide accrediting agencies. The proliferation of bogus schools and accrediting agencies creates confusion and problems for the traditional profit-making schools spreading throughout our nation. The question that is frequently being raised is "Why are profit-making schools spreading so fast?" Private corporations such as Edison Schools, Inc., National Heritage Academies, and Advantage Schools claim they can offer a host of innovations and attain academic success for less than it costs to provide public education. Profit-making corporations have contracted with public schools to administer the school system or particular schools. Furthermore, they appear to be attractive to parents because they give parents another choice and claim they can deliver quality education.

Postsecondary vocational skills are often abusing taxpayers and their students by falsifying student loan applications and then providing little in the way of meaningful skills and knowledge to them. We are witnessing today a degree of charlatanism in education that is unprecedented. Why? The answer is easy: Education is a huge industry, and many see it as a way to get their hands on the almighty buck.

It is no secret that many public schools are failing, and profit-making education companies are responding to this failure by offering an alternative. The success of for-profit schools is still open for discussion. However, these schools claim they have efficient administrative procedures and have greater freedom in teacher recruitment and retention. Critics claim that profit-making schools cut corners, do not offer comprehensive programs such as special education, and limit the number of athletic activities. These data, according to the critics, do not substantiate success, especially in disadvantaged communities. The authors are also skeptics that profit-making schools are willing to make the financial investment to provide comprehensive education superior to public schools.

Finally, the oldest and most successful competing institutions to public schools have been private and religious schools. Although all three are traditional conveyors of education, private and religious schools have gained momentum during the past several decades. There is a growing reluctance by many parents to send their children to public schools.

There are distinct differences among public, private, and religious schools. It appears that more and more parents are seeing advantages to having their children attend private and religious schools in that they do not have to contend with a large educational bureaucracy that makes the public school system impersonal.

Parents also feel that the public schools ignore religious topics, do not celebrate religious holidays, and do not promote the values they cherish. Some parents believe that the teacher unions exert too much influence and that they are too involved in political debate. Parents contend that very few tenured teachers who fail to fulfill their duties are dismissed, and there is little accountability, in general, by teachers or administrators. There is also a perception that the availability of drugs, lack of safety, and a high dropout rate exists in the public schools. Finally, the question of textbook selection, curriculum development, and class size all contribute to parents' preferring the nonpublic education sector.

The pros and cons of public schools versus nonpublic schools will continue for decades. However, there is a deep concern by all parents that their children have outstanding teachers, high-quality programs, and a quality learning environment, free of violence. These factors have contributed to this fierce competition.

Competition in the educational arena is welcomed by the authors, but not at the expense of quality. Opening new doors to the traditional educational delivery systems needs to be encouraged and welcomed, yet safeguards need to be introduced, pilot programs should be carefully scrutinized, periodic audits need to be undertaken, and accountability and objective measures of success need to be established. Most importantly, teachers cannot be expected to teach effectively unless the classroom is violence-free.

KEY QUESTIONS FOR TEACHERS

1. How do you feel about homeschooling versus the traditional school?
2. What do you think is the effect of the voucher system on the public schools?
3. What is your opinion regarding public funds going to religious schools?
4. Is there a place in our society for charter schools?
5. Do you think that profit-making schools should be required to offer the same courses as public schools?
6. Should religion be part of the public school curriculum? What about the teaching of values?
7. What influence do you feel class size has on education?
8. Would the schools be better off if tenure would not be given to any teachers?
9. Would teacher quality be improved if all teachers were subjected to a quality review of their work and ranked according to a standard?

II

THE TEACHER
AND THE MARKETPLACE

4

THE PROFESSIONAL PREPARATION OF TEACHERS: WHAT IS THE REMEDY?

The classroom teacher is the most important individual in the educational delivery process. Observers of the educational scene and the literature oftentimes focus on the importance of the principal as the instructional leader and on the superintendent as the policy originator and implementer. These views may be accurate but, in the end, the delivery of educational services is almost totally dependent on the individual responsible for the direct instruction to students in a classroom setting.

Concerns about the quality of services delivered by teachers have led to the creation of many programs, some of which actually script what a teacher says and does during the time he or she interacts with children. Such scripting is doomed to failure—although it will be hailed as a success before it is discarded. It is the fate of all educational innovations to be "doomed to success" before they disappear, usually to reappear a few decades later with a new name and presented as the "new, can't-miss solution" to the same problems that still ail us. Thus, is it any wonder that most teachers are highly cynical about the latest can't-miss educational program introduced to guarantee the success of the children in their classrooms?

The fact that there is so much concern about the quality of teachers in the United States reflects the importance of the position. Today, the preparation of teachers is still mainly the responsibility of schools of education within colleges and universities. Schools of education award credits and degrees to students who then can redeem them at state education departments in order to qualify for certification as a teacher. This monopoly is now threatened by teacher unions, which want to have the right to offer credit-bearing courses that would be accepted by the state education departments. Entrepreneurial ventures, such as Stanley Kaplan, Inc., which formerly offered test preparation courses to students, are now in the business of offering graduate credits. Basically, college and university teacher education programs stand accused of doing a lousy job in preparing teachers.

Teachers come in all shapes, sizes, and colors. What we do know with certainty is that research overwhelmingly shows that individuals who aspire to become teachers do not score high on SATs and that most education programs are not challenging their students. Sad to say, in our society, there are too many individuals who go into teaching as a major in college because they do not know what else they want to do or because there are certain perks to the job, such as a 180-day work year, tenure, and an outstanding compensation package that includes medical benefits and pension plans.

Further complicating the problem of preparing outstanding teachers is the fact that very few education majors are dropped from the program once they have begun. Keep in mind that universities and colleges are businesses. They are driven by enrollments and the bottom line. One could debate whether schools of education are less rigorous than other components of higher education, but the bottom line is that few students are dropped from teacher preparation programs. Higher enrollments mean more classes, more classes mean more faculty positions.

Upon completion of an undergraduate teacher education program, most individuals are eligible for a provisional teaching certificate. Presently, under the No Child Left Behind Act (NCLB), the goal is to have a fully certified teacher in every classroom in the United States and that such a teacher should be certified in the subject area in which he or she is teaching. Don't hold your breath for this to happen.

Certainly, critics of teacher preparation programs can have a field day criticizing those programs. We are probably not exceptions to that rule. On the other hand, we are not running for political office, state superintendent of schools, or some other political or educational decision-making office. From our vantage point, based on over 150 years among the three of us in observing schools and the personnel in them, we can draw certain conclusions that are just as applicable today as they have been for the past 50 years.

Schools and school systems are easy targets for critics. Sometimes, we bring these criticisms on ourselves. Fifty years ago, some school systems required all teacher applicants to be conversant in English and to speak without an accent in grammatically correct usage. As the teacher shortage deepened in the 1950s, there were calls to relax these speech standards. These calls coincided with black and Latino, mostly Mexican and Puerto Rican, children increasingly replacing Caucasian youngsters in urban school systems in the United States. Consequently, supporters of relaxing teaching standards cited the example of Albert Einstein, whom they claimed would fail an examination to become a physics teacher in an urban high school because he had a German accent. A little later, the flood of black and Latino youngsters into urban schools brought calls for more minority teachers, particularly for those conversant in Spanish, to service such students. The belief was that minority teachers could more effectively educate minority youngsters. Such views went largely un-challenged, although there was no core of research to support such a view.

There was also the issue raised by some that it was inherently racist to advocate the lowering of speech standards so that more minority indi-viduals could become teachers. Certainly, to a large degree, we are all products of our environment—yet we can all strive to improve. The re-laxation—and in some cases, the abolition—of any speech standards in order to become a teacher did result in teachers with difficulties in En-glish teaching students who also had difficulties in English. In some cases, the solution to that problem was to simply do away with the teach-ing of English or to modify the English language itself. Examples of this were the creation of non-English-speaking classes and bilingual classes, almost exclusively populated by Latino youngsters. Supposedly, young-sters were to be in these classes until they learned English. For most, however, placement in such classes was permanent, with very few stu-dents ever leaving them for the English-speaking classes. If African American students did not speak English very well, the answer to that problem could be found by simply teaching them in "street lingo," referred to as Ebonics. Black children experiencing learning difficulties now could find school boards that changed the method of instruction so that such children were educated in black idiomatic language. This is what happened in Oakland, California, and several other large, heavily populated African American school systems.

Such solutions are scams, usually run by scam artists, who usually try to maintain their own positions or political base by advocating such hoaxes. The bottom line was, despite the national publicity, Ebonics did not work. It did not improve the learning of black youngsters. One of the dirty little secrets of education is that even the most well-meaning, knowledgeable educators do not know what will be effective with children. They cannot say this publicly, but it is the truth. We can tell you that there is no easy cure for the learning problems that ail millions of youngsters attending schools in the United States today. We can also tell you with certainty that there is no educational innovation that will work for all youngsters, although some will work for a few youngsters.

In the 1980s, the New Jersey state superintendent of schools stated that requirements to become a teacher in that state should be modified to allow physics majors who graduated from Princeton to become teachers. The state superintendent pointed out that not one physics major who graduated from Princeton had become a teacher, due to the influence of schools of education on the certification process. Subsequently, certification regulations were changed to allow for a period of time for certification requirements to be met *after* one had begun to teach. As far as we know, no physics major from Princeton decided to become a teacher after the certification requirements were changed—making this just one more hoax.

We do not believe that courses and credits, in and of themselves, automatically make for good teachers. Teaching is an art, and great teachers are artists. As in most other fields of endeavor, from medicine to working behind the counter at McDonald's, people bring different motivations and abilities to their tasks. Teaching is no different. For every Derek Jeter, there are three players of average ability. Most teachers are average. There are some great ones but also those who should have never been admitted to teacher education programs. If such individuals go on to become teachers and do not improve in their performance,

they should be weeded out of the profession. We recognize that certification rules of various states should not prohibit capable individuals
from becoming teachers.

Recently, there has been a discussion as to why holders of doctorates
in various subjects must meet state teacher certification requirements.
After all, doesn't a doctorate signify ability in a given subject area? The
problem is more complex than it appears. Yes, the holder of a doctorate
in medieval English literature focusing on Chaucer may indeed be
knowledgeable of Chaucer, but does that enable such an individual to
teach the broad range of content covered in English classes? There are
no guarantees. There are doctoral holders who have the gift and desire
to be great teachers and there are those who do not possess such gifts.
The great teacher not only knows his or her subject area but is also able
to convey what he or she knows to children in a manner that enables
them to grasp what the teacher is presenting. To a large degree, no
teacher education program can instill its graduates with the gift of liking
students or liking their job.

Those of us who have taught know that teaching effectively is an ex-
cruciatingly difficult task. We often hear that "every child can learn." To
an extent, this canard is a public relations gimmick. Of course, every
child can learn, but don't delude yourself—not every child can learn
equally well. Not every child can learn material in the same time period
as other children. Not every child has unlimited capacity to learn. Our
view is that every child can learn basic skills to become a contributing
member of American society. We do not believe that every child has the
ability to earn a PhD in physics or history. Anyone who tells you differently is perpetuating the "hoax."

Teaching is difficult because so few of us have the special gift to impart what we know to what children want to know. Since most of us fall
into the average category on the normal distribution curve, teaching
methodology does become important in the sense that there are techniques and methods that can improve effectiveness in delivering educational services.

As we have seen from the collapse of Enron, hoaxes are not restricted
to education. Despite the calls for certified teachers in every classroom
and for improving the quality of teachers, this will not occur as long
as there are teacher shortages in specific subject areas and in specific

geographic areas. One of the basic rules of administering a school, one a smart principal learns quickly, is that every classroom must have a "body," called a teacher, in front of the classroom. In some geographic areas, the shortage of teachers is so dire that the body in front of the classroom need not even be a warm body. In some cases, even a cold body will do.

Keep the above in mind as we discuss trends on the preparation of teachers in the remainder of this chapter. Education is not a science. When Jonas Salk discovered a cure for polio, it worked for the entire population. Most research studies on best practices and methodologies in education, however, are often contradictory. For example, studies are contradictory as to whether students learn more from fully certified teachers than they do from those teaching with emergency or provisional certification. Some research indicates that there is no evidence that individuals not fully certified were less effective in teaching students and colleagues who are fully certified. On the other hand, studies by David Berliner and Linda Darling-Hammond indicate that the opposite is true. The National Board for Professional Teaching Standards, whose existence is largely owed to Albert Shanker, the late president of the American Federation of Teachers (AFT), has tried to improve teacher quality by offering advance certification for teachers in a style similar to what the medical profession offers to doctors. The question that remains largely unanswered, however, is: Are such certified teachers bringing about improvements in student achievement? We believe in the importance of permanently certified teachers.

It should always be kept in mind that high quality is not synonymous with highly qualified. Qualified means possessing the credentials necessary to secure the position. Quality means producing substantive results once that position is secured. In Massachusetts, teachers had to pass a fluency test in English, as approved in a ballot measure approved by Massachusetts voters. The measure called for the replacement of bilingual classes with English immersion classes and that teachers of bilingual classes should be required to pass an exam that would attest to their fluency and literacy in English. Consequently, some teachers who failed the exam have been either laid off or terminated. Subsequent legal action and the need for bodies in the classroom resulted in the affected individuals being offered additional opportunities to pass the examination.

In many large cities, securing a teaching position has become a bureaucratic, dehumanizing mess. New York City has been the model example of such a situation, going back many years. Many large cities assign a license or certification number to prospective employees, who are then subjected to long waits and complex hiring rules before licensure is granted. Given the difficulty that prospective teachers encounter in securing a position, is it any surprise that there is such a high turnover in the first 5 years in the professional lives of teachers? Some argue that the actual on-the-job experiences of new teachers actually sort out those individuals who should have been screened out by schools of education in the first place. Charles Darwin called this "survival of the fittest." On the other hand, there are those who say that the high turnover among new teachers is due to the difficulty of the job, the failure of colleges to adequately train effective teachers, and the lack of support new teachers get from their school administration, colleagues, and teacher organizations.

Obviously, one way of possibly attracting better candidates into the teaching profession is to offer them higher salaries. Such calls from educational reformers are standard and are usually accompanied by calls for commensurate increases in teacher accountability. Let's be frank. In many suburban areas in particular, teachers are well paid. Not only are they well paid in some cases, but they also have attractive total compensation packages. Fringe benefits for teachers are now exceeding fringe benefits available to mid-management types in the corporate sector. For example, IBM and CBS have recently significantly revised their pension plans so as to make employees largely responsible for their own pension via 401(k) plans. Many educators, however, and other civil service employees have attractive pension plans that enable them to retire at the age of 55 or to vest in their pension plans after 10 years of service. They have attractive medical plans, college tuition plans, and, upon retirement after 25 or 30 years of service, receive pensions that include a significant proportion of what they earned when employed, as well as retaining their medical coverage. It is not that we are against higher salaries for teachers, but to couple such calls with greater teacher accountability is nonsense.

What is it then that we advocate for improving the preparation and quality of teachers? First, standards for admission into the field must be raised. If one could become a medical doctor as easily as one could become a teacher, there would be very little confidence in the medical profession. Let us start by advocating stronger programs at the college level for prospective teachers. Given the great inflation that exists in colleges throughout the country, it would not be unfair to require a minimum of 2.9 to 3.0 GPA for admission into a teacher education program. Prospective teachers should have to pass a written examination demonstrating competency with the English language in such areas as sentence structure, spelling, punctuation, and grammar.

Teacher education programs should emphasize field-based training. The majority of time should be spent in schools, supplemented by strong, high-quality classroom instruction. There should be a weeding out of poor students from the programs. Not everyone who is admitted to a teacher education program should graduate. Faculty observations of prospective teachers must certainly be concerned with improving performance, but if such improvement does not occur, it should result in the prospective teacher being dropped from the program. Such observations should take place at least every 2 weeks for two semesters. After these two semesters, one should not expect a master teacher, but one does have the right to expect someone to whom the university is giving a stamp of approval to go into a classroom and perform in a competent manner.

Upon securing employment, a teacher must be closely supervised by the administrators in a school. Since most teachers are now governed by collective bargaining contracts, administrators must be aware of the do's and don'ts of their particular contract. Administrators must be imbued with the philosophy that improving the classroom performance of their new teachers and the high-quality performance of their experienced teachers is their most important task. In school districts where there are many more applicants than there are positions available, administrators should maintain the philosophy that if a new teacher is no more than "okay," then that teacher should be replaced. The law of supply and demand should require this. Why settle for okay when there is the potential for excellence? In urban areas and in other places where there is a shortage of teachers, okay may have to do. We hate to say this, but this is a reality. On the other hand, regardless of the need for teachers, ineffective new teachers should be terminated before they are awarded tenure.

The two large teacher organizations in this country, the AFT and National Education Association (NEA), have become a force in the world of education. Both organizations are now trying to expand their role in the preparation of teachers. They have both made a mark already in providing in-service training for teachers already on the job. Having said that, both organizations must continue to see that the due process provisions of teacher contracts are fulfilled, but they should not become roadblocks to improving the standards for entry into or remaining in the teaching profession. In the long run, it is in their best interest to be viewed by the general pubic as supporters of higher qualifications for admission into the profession, rather than as roadblocks to increasing the quality of teachers.

Graduate schools of education must be more discerning in their admissions policies and graduation requirements. We believe the general public would be shocked if they knew the actual rate of acceptance into master's degree programs in graduate schools of education around the country.

State education departments must stop playing games about accrediting institutions with little or no full-time faculty that offer graduate and undergraduate degrees. Such institutions are more concerned with the business of education than they are in producing quality educators. There is a difference between earning a master's degree from the Wharton School of Business of the University of Pennsylvania and earning an MBA from Podunk University. In education, however, it does not seem to matter what school a student attends in order to meet state certification requirements. State departments of education must increase certification requirements, require subject and basic literacy examinations with real scoring standards, and close down institutions within their states that consistently put out poor graduates. We are not optimistic that this can occur, given the power of vested interest groups supporting the status quo. As a result, who will suffer? The children will!

KEY QUESTIONS FOR TEACHERS

1. Should all teacher preparation colleges be evaluated?
2. Do you believe that a minimum standard should be set for all teachers?

3. Should teachers be allowed to teach if they have not met minimum standards?
4. Should teacher preparation only be offered at the graduate level?
5. Teachers are allowed to teach "out of license" in many states. Do you believe this should be allowed?
6. Some people believe that teacher preparation should take into account the personality of the candidate. Do you agree?
7. Schools of education differ according to the standards of admission. Should all teachers nationally meet a minimum standard?
8. There are some theorists who believe that, because someone knows his subject matter very well, he would be a good teacher. Do you agree?
9. Who should certify teachers? A national board or a state agency?
10. How much of a voice should teachers have in certification policies?

5

JOB HUNTING AND MOBILITY: WHAT SHOULD YOU KNOW?

Once an individual has graduated from college and has at least earned provisional certification as a teacher, the "fun" of finding a position begins. Teaching positions can be abundant or scarce. Data concerning teacher supply and demand must be disaggregated into specific subject areas and certification areas in order to be meaningful. For example, wealthy suburbs surrounding most of the large cities of our nation can oftentimes have hundreds of applicants for a few teaching vacancies as elementary school teachers and as teachers of English and social studies. On the other hand, the same school districts can have difficulty attracting teachers certified in mathematics, the sciences, and special education.

Over the years, the authors have received many thank-you notes from students who think we secured positions for them as teachers and administrators. We have always insisted that this was never the case. We have yet to get anybody a job. What we have been able to do was to facilitate interviews for various vacancies. This is not difficult to do since, over time, many of our master's and doctoral degree graduates eventually moved into leadership positions in schools and school districts. We have also been very fortunate in that the students enrolled in the universities in which we worked throughout the country attracted many top-notch potential teachers. If we believed in the capabilities of an individual seeking a position and our assistance, then we had no hesitation calling school and district leaders to recommend such outstanding applicants. On many occasions, such calls or conversations would result in the job applicant receiving an interview.

Once our candidate was called for an interview, our work was done. They either got the job or did not get the job, based on how they performed in the interview process and their overall qualifications. The hiring process may not only involve an interview but may also require a candidate to teach a class in the district while being observed by district administrators. The candidate must face several hurdles that are independent of our recommendations. Thus, we believed that we never got anyone a job—but, on the other hand, sound recommendations are essential prerequisites for obtaining positions in the field of education.

Online postings for vacancies are now critical for job seekers to review. These online postings have probably now exceeded the importance of local newspapers, educational journals, and newspapers as the most important vehicle for finding a teaching position. Our recommendation is that, if you see a position you think you are qualified to fill, then apply for it. Keep in mind that, by law, teaching vacancies must be advertised. Such advertisements do not always guarantee that the position is actually vacant. Many times, a candidate for the position has been selected before the vacancy is posted. The person selected may be someone who is substituting at that particular school and doing a good job. Another possibility is that an individual may have been assigned to a school as a student teacher, did an excellent job, and now that there is a vacancy, may have the so-called "inside track" for the position. Let us not forget another possibility: A vacancy may be filled by an individual who is "wired" to various members of the school district's decision-making circle.

We were reminded of this by a 2006 story in the *New York Times* that described how a teacher in a New Jersey school district had been caught kissing and groping a 13-year-old male. When the principal of her school asked the superintendent to fire the teacher, she was instead promoted to guidance counselor at the local high school. The principal simply assumed that because the teacher in question had a father who was well-connected in the town's business and political life, there was nothing more that he could do. Eventually this guidance counselor became pregnant by an 11th grader at the high school and married him upon his graduation. Later, a 15-year-old moved in with the teacher and her husband, and this teenager later filed a complaint of statutory rape against the teacher. The matter was settled when the school district allowed the teacher to take an early retirement package and even sponsored a retirement party for her! What are we saying? That knowing the right people can not only keep one out of trouble but also help find a position. However, please remember that the best policy is to do the right thing and use common sense.

The No Child Left Behind Act (NCLB) calls for teachers to possess a bachelor's degree, permanent state teacher's certification, and have demonstrated competence in the subject for which they are certified. Throughout the country, compliance with NCLB varies dramatically. Once again, high-socioeconomic-status school districts will have a much greater proportion of their teachers meeting those requirements than would inner-city school districts located in places like Washington, D.C., Cleveland, Detroit, Houston, Philadelphia, and Baltimore. It should also be remembered that states in which these cities are located may differ markedly as to what state education departments require for certification.

Depending on the socioeconomic status of a school system, the vacancy rate should be about 10% annually. Vacancies occur through retirement and by teachers simply finding that life as a teacher is too difficult and demanding. What attracts individuals into teaching will vary significantly. Some are attracted to the notion of performing in a position that leaves a societal legacy. Others are attracted by the short work year and workday. Others are attracted by the job security aspect of teaching. There are also factors such as retiring at age 55, vesting after 10 years, and generous fringe packages, including pensions and medical benefits. Many teachers are surprised at how demanding and difficult it is to teach children. Albert Shanker used to ask parents how difficult it was to control their own two or three children. He then asked them to imagine how difficult it is for a teacher to supervise and educate 30 to 40 children. Indeed, we believe that Shanker's illustration was an apt one.

Teachers who wish to change jobs or are looking for their first assign-ment should not hesitate to apply to as many positions as they wish. Some applicants are hesitant to submit multiple applications. We en-courage you to do so. Never be worried that your application may be turned down. So what?! The marketplace is an open arena, and you should feel free to avail yourself of all opportunities. Very few personnel officers will admit that many jobs are obtained through friends and spe-cial contacts.

You should carefully prepare for your job interview. Dress appropri-ately, and do not minimize good grooming. You should be cognizant of your diction and language usage. Do not interrupt the interviewer. Be calm and under control. Listen to the questions carefully. Do not ram-ble in your replies. Be organized with your thoughts. Give a calm, thoughtful impression. Be polite, and express thanks for the opportunity to be interviewed.

Job hunting and mobility should not be left to chance. Careful prepa-ration and thought should be given to the following questions:

- In what geographical area of the country do I want to teach?
- At what level do I want to teach?
- Do I want to teach in a private, religious, or public school?
- What are my salary expectations?
- What about the school's academic reputation?
- What is included in the school and faculty handbooks?
- Does the school have a homework policy?
- Will I belong to a pension plan?
- What are my fringe benefits?
- At what time do I report to work?
- At what time do teachers leave the school premises?
- Is there a teacher's union?
- What are the dues?
- Is there a published salary scale?
- Are sabbaticals available to the faculty?
- Who will evaluate my job performance?
- How often will I have a job performance conference?

Do not be discouraged if you fail to obtain a desired teaching post. Keep looking, and never take a rejection personally. In our own careers, on more than a few occasions, we failed to be chosen for the position we sought.

Good luck to you. We are confident that if you prepare an attractive biographical statement, obtain excellent references, achieve solid grades in your undergraduate and graduate studies, and give a good impression in your interview, you will be successful in finding a suitable position.

However, you must keep in mind that supply and demand play an important part in your success. As already indicated, some teaching disciplines have a greater need than others. Therefore, if you are in an area with an excess of teacher applicants, your chances of obtaining your preferred school or location may be diminished. Nevertheless, do not give up your hunt!

KEY QUESTIONS FOR TEACHERS

1. Do you think that the number of courses you have taken in your teaching subject area places you at an advantage in obtaining a teaching position?
2. What strategies would you develop if you were to apply for a teaching position?
3. Should you practice with a colleague or friend prior to interviewing for a teaching position?
4. In preparing for an interview, what are the advantages of learning as much as possible about the school system and community before the interview?
5. If you were interviewing for a highly competitive teaching position, what advantages do you bring to the position?
6. What do you believe are the advantages of teaching in a private school, religious school, or public school? Which do you prefer?
7. In an interview, do you think it is appropriate to initiate discussion on your salary?

8. If you disagree with the curriculum of the school in which you are seeking a position, should you bring this up during an interview?
9. What questions do you think it appropriate for you to ask during an interview?
10. Should you be concerned in the interview about parent-teacher relationships and what the school policies are on this matter?

6

MERIT PAY: HAS ITS DAY ARRIVED?

Merit pay is one of those issues that have a serious impact on the teaching profession. It is a concept that has been around for decades, often submerged by other "new solutions," but is again a prime topic of discussion in educational circles. In its simplest form, merit pay is a system to pay some teachers more money and/or provide other forms of compensation as a reward for a perceived higher level of performance based on criteria that spark controversy and disagreement.

The controversy surrounding merit pay is a longstanding one. It was a suggested educational reform even before the first collective bargaining contract for teachers was negotiated in New York City in 1961. Prior to that date, many teachers opposed merit pay because they thought it would give principals unbridled power to reward their "cronies" without any input from teachers and would be based on criteria that they claimed were never clear. Merit pay provokes strong feelings and is a hotly debated issue both among educators and lay people.

Since the advent of collective bargaining in 1961 and its rapid spread throughout the country, teacher organizations traditionally opposed merit pay as being undemocratic. Lately, however, they have softened their stance. By softening, we mean that teacher organizations, through their local affiliates, now want to be the key component in determining the criteria for merit pay and in deciding who should receive it. It is difficult to precisely gauge teacher attitudes toward merit pay. Rank-and-file teachers are concerned that favoritism would creep into the decision-making process. That may well be true. However, if teachers were meaningfully involved in the selection process, it is our belief that a greater number of teachers would support merit pay.

The concept of rewarding teachers for performance above and beyond the norm is neither a new one, nor is it without imperfections. Identifying which teachers are the best ones does not involve Einsteinian laws of physics. All teachers in a given school know which of their colleagues are of the highest caliber and which ones are of the lowest caliber. The universal litmus test for this phenomenon would be to simply ask any teacher in a school whom they would want to teach their own child. Even student interns or newly appointed teachers to a school know within a matter of a few weeks what all the other teachers in the school already know—who are the best teachers. This litmus test is unerringly accurate. Teachers also know who are the worst teachers among them—those they would never allow to teach their very own children.

Historically, the reward system for teachers was predicated on moving out of the position of classroom teacher into a position as guidance counselor, school psychologist, assistant/vice principal, or principal. Such a move was usually accompanied by a pay increase from what one earned as a teacher. Today, however, there is some reluctance on the part of many teachers to leave their positions. They see the enormous pressure placed on administrators: an 11-month work year when most teachers are working a 180-day school calendar; the loss of one's tenure rights as a teacher by moving to an administrative position; and the ever-greater involvement of parents in the day-to-day operations of schools that is placing more limitations on the decision-making ability of school leaders while increasing the pressures brought to bear on them by legislation such as the No Child Left Behind Act (NCLB), with its emphasis on testing and accountability.

In the world of business, commerce, and sports, recognition of different levels of performance and rewarding outstanding performance via salary increases is a given. In teaching and in most other civil service areas, however, salaries are predicated solely on years of experience in the field and the number of graduate credits accumulated. To give an example of how out of step opposition to merit pay can be, think of Michael Jordan, after 5 years of playing for the Chicago Bulls in the National Basketball Association, being paid the same salary as every other NBA player with 5 years of experience; most would say this is very unfair. Michael Jordan should not be paid the same salary as others with similar experience because he has performed at a higher level sufficient to entitle him to much greater remuneration. If this is what you think, we would agree with you. Yet this is exactly what happens in the field of education among teachers.

Like every other system devised to improve on a problem, merit pay is not without its flaws. It will never be foolproof. In the recent past, merit pay systems have been introduced into various school systems, and teachers unworthy of receiving merit pay nevertheless were recipients. It should also be remembered that, in and of itself, merit pay will not solve all of the educational ills confronting our schools. We do believe, however, that it is a step in the right direction.

Many pluses and minuses would come into play if a merit pay system was to be implemented. Let us repeat that the implementation of a merit pay system will not automatically solve the problems dogging education today in many areas of the country. We can say with certainty that merit pay will not make schools safer places for children. Classrooms will not become less overcrowded. It will not end the problems created by social promotion. It will not make parents more interested in their children's school progress in school systems where they are passive, or less involved in systems in which they are hyperinvolved.

In our minds, the broad adoption of merit pay would let prospective teachers, and even those who are remotely contemplating careers in education, know that they will not be locked to a salary predicated solely on years of experience and number of graduate credits. This may result in attracting brighter and more adventurous college students to the field of education. It is often not true that the best teachers in the school were those who had the highest grade point averages while in college. On the other hand, we might be able to do without those teachers who constantly misspell words on the board and are really academically unfit to mold the minds of children in grades K–12. It should also be made clear that we do not believe that teachers who earn merit pay will work harder because of receiving this recognition. Those teachers who truly deserve merit pay are usually those already working at maximum capacity without merit pay. We do believe, however, that teachers working at 80 to 90% of maximum effort will work even harder if a monetary incentive were given as a reward for such efforts. This could lead to the improvement in the general, overall quality of teaching and, consequently, in the improvement of pupil learning.

Many critics of merit pay have focused on the issue that merit recipients will be those teachers whose pupils score the highest on standardized tests, which, in the eyes of such critics, does not define actual learning. Critics also focus on how merit pay would create divisive competition, ill will, and jealousy among the professional staff in the school. This, they believe, would diminish trust, collaboration, and shared accountability among teachers. Certainly, there is a possibility of this occurring. On the other hand, most private and some public universities in the United States have been using a merit pay system for many years. This does not seem to have had a negative impact on the way such universities are viewed both in the United States and around the world. It seems to us that, as much as our nation's K–12 schools are reviled, the very opposite is true in the way the quality of our colleges and universities are perceived worldwide. If there is competition among professors, it is not because of merit pay. If there is lack of trust and collaboration among college faculty, it is not because of merit pay. Is the merit pay system in those colleges and universities where it is in use foolproof? Of course not! No system presently in operation in education is perfect. By and large, however, the system seems to work more often than not.

A closer examination of college/university merit systems reveals certain common characteristics. Merit, by definition, refers to performance beyond simply being competent. The awarding of merit pay is usually restricted to a maximum of anywhere between 20 and 60% of the eligible group. The merit pay award itself can vary anywhere from an average of $1,000 to $5,000 per year. This award then becomes a permanent part of that faculty member's base salary. Thus, there is a financial incentive for university personnel to strive for a merit pay award. In the colleges and universities where merit pay seems to work best, there are clear criteria for receiving the award. Even in these places, however, the established merit pay criteria can still be unclear. We have also found that, even if the merit pay award is a pittance, faculty get a psychological lift from being singled out as a recipient. This is probably due to the fact that most universities where merit pay is in operation depend heavily on the recommendation of fellow faculty who serve on merit pay committees. Thus, peer recognition and the awarding of 15 cents or $1,500 plays a major role in motivating faculty to qualify for merit pay. However, the final decision on awarding merit still usually rests with school and university administrators.

In higher education, three areas are frequently cited as being the ones in which faculty must perform beyond the norm. These are areas of research and publication, teaching, and service to the university and community. Although subdivisions within these three categories can be controversial and a source of contention, there is no doubt that merit pay for teachers of grades K–12 should focus heavily on classroom teaching performance. Consequently, there must be a level of trust among the teaching staff if merit pay is to truly work in a fair and honest manner. What would be the criteria to judge excellent teaching? Who would determine these criteria? Who would evaluate if the criteria had been sufficiently achieved? Would student test scores be a valid measure for receiving merit pay? How would the actual process of awarding merit pay work? Should administrators, parents, and students have a voice as to which teachers should receive a merit pay award? Should the merit pay award list be made public? Should it be made available in rank order?

All of these questions are not easily answered. For example, it is our belief that whether or not a district's policy would be to keep a list of merit pay recipients confidential, the names will eventually leak out. Then it could be argued that all the parents would descend on the principal's office to ensure that their child was placed in the classes of teachers who received merit pay awards. We also know, however, that even without a merit pay system there is a network of parental "buzz," usually gathered from older siblings or neighbors, about the competence or incompetence of specific teachers in a given school. We would be ignoring reality if we did not acknowledge that, even without a merit pay system in place many parents descend on principals' offices demanding specific teachers for their children.

Ramon Cortines, former chancellor of the New York City school system, wanted to link the pay of teachers to the test results achieved by their students when he was the interim superintendent of the Los Angeles school district. Denver (Colorado) teachers approved a pilot program that would have given bonuses to teachers if their students met specified goals for academic performance. In one of the most publicized merit pay programs, the Fairfax County (Virginia) school district, one of the largest in the nation, attempted to give annual bonuses of up to $1,000 to those teachers who scored at the top of the district's evaluation system. This was after the same school district had voted to abolish a merit pay system.

Albert Shanker, the late, great labor leader and educational statesman, publicly proclaimed in 1989 that educators needed to transform their schools into achievement-oriented institutions or be faced with alternatives that might put them out of business. Among the reforms Shanker advocated was the acceptance of a merit pay system that would reward outstanding teachers. Earlier that year, Mary Futrell, then president of the National Education Association (NEA), publicly lauded the work of a local NEA affiliate in Fairfax County in devising a performance-based pay plan for teachers in that district.

On the other hand, the death of Shanker and the void created by the subsequent absence of bold teacher union leaders have resulted in slow, if any, progress in the area of merit pay awards. Local teacher union affiliates, in such places New York City and elsewhere, often hint at their willingness to accept merit pay awards. Such "willingness" seems to be more of a tease and a public relations ploy to show parents and taxpayers that teacher unions are not automatically opposed to all educational reforms.

Prior to 1989, Shanker had noted that hundreds of merit pay programs were adopted by school boards during the decades before teachers were unionized and, with very few exceptions, all were abandoned—not because of the organized power of teachers, which did not exist in those days, but because of the negative impact merit pay plans had on morale and on the efficient functioning of schools. Shanker's observation was accurate. The authors maintain, however, that merit pay, even with its warts, is still preferable to a salary schedule that does not recognize variations in effective teacher performance.

We believe that monetary incentives will motivate large numbers of teachers to not only strive for the cash reward but also provide them with the psychological sense of satisfaction growing out of their inner need to achieve recognition for excellence. Monetary incentives might serve to attract individuals into the field of teaching who would not have the civil service mentality of "It doesn't matter how hard I work, everybody gets the same pay increase." This mentality is unhealthy, pervasive in some school systems, and does not benefit children in the teaching and learning process. Merit pay would also send a signal to parents and taxpayers that educators are serious about tying salaries to performance. As teacher salaries rise across the board, so do school taxes. One need not be ultrasensitive to realize that there is a growing uneasiness among both taxpayers and parents about the quality of services delivered by teachers in classrooms that, at the same time, is accompanied by escalating costs. Certainly, one of the reasons for the flight of many middle-class citizens from the northeastern section of the United States to the warmer-climate states of this country is the "pull" of much lower school taxes. Don't believe for a moment that it is only the warmer weather that is luring people from the Northeast.

The adoption of a merit pay system would send a message to parents that educators are serious about improving performance in public schools. Shanker once said that the very existence of public schools was threatened by the adoption of a voucher system, as parents would then be able to take their children out of the pubic schools and put them in private schools. This observation has very sad implications. Are public schools only to educate the children of the poorer urban, suburban, and rural populations? Children should not remain "captives" to public schools systems simply because they do not have the financial means to enroll elsewhere.

Educators and critics of merit pay make some very good points in citing weaknesses of this model. They are correct when they point out that creating objective, measurable, and relevant criteria for receiving merit pay can be an extraordinarily difficult process. Such critics are also correct when they say that the ranking of merit pay applicants could turn out to be highly subjective. We have no doubt that, in some situations, this will be true. Merit pay can also lead to negative morale among teachers who do not receive such awards. After all, the total amount of dollars allocated toward salary increases is not going to increase if a merit pay system is adopted. Rather, we envision a system in which the available amount for salary increases will be reallocated. Across-the-board increases will continue, but they will be less than in the past because a proportion of the money for salary increases will now be utilized for merit pay awards.

In determining who would receive merit pay, we certainly envision school administrators, teachers (and we don't mean just union activists), parents, and, in some cases, even children being involved. Student test scores could be one valid criterion for receiving merit pay but certainly not the only criteria. Otherwise, merit pay awards would be tilted toward teachers who teach the brightest children. Not all children can show month-to-month learning progress as measured by tests. On the other hand, there are classes in which children enter already far behind in basic skills, yet make progress, even if it is at times slow progress, as a result of the extraordinary efforts of teachers.

Some argue that the introduction of a merit system would strain relationships among teachers and between teachers and the school administration. Those of us who spend time in schools are often struck by the already poor morale among teachers and between teachers and the school administration. These observations are made in schools that do not have a merit pay system. Let's not kid ourselves: Critics of merit pay have some valid points, but the real basis for their opposition is their fear of change. We cannot guarantee that the adoption of a merit pay system will enhance learning. As we look at many school systems, however, we see schools that have produced generations of dropouts, failures, and individuals with asocial behavior. Are the schools solely responsible for this? Of course not! Yet we must come back to our basic premise: We must try new things not because we know they will work but because there is a possibility that they may work better than the system now in place. What have we got to lose?

In addition to improved student performance, merit pay criteria should include:

- Teacher attendance
- Volunteering for additional professional development
- Willingness to teach difficult classes

- Willingness to teach larger classes
- The quality of teacher–student interaction
- The extent and quality of contacts with parents and other members of the community or other organizations and institutions therein

Accountability should exist for teachers as well as students. Merit pay is certainly one concept whose implementation would bring accountability for teachers a step closer to reality.

KEY QUESTIONS FOR TEACHERS

1. Do you think merit pay would increase the quality of teaching?
2. Is it possible for merit pay to be awarded objectively?
3. If a teacher does not earn merit pay, does it mean that this teacher should be terminated?
4. What criteria do you think should be used in awarding merit pay?
5. What effect do you think merit pay would have on teachers not given merit pay?
6. What impact might the awarding or denial of merit pay have on parents in a school community?
7. Would you object to teachers' earning more pay because of a merit system? Would the unions object? What would the effect be on morale?
8. Should tenure be given only to those teachers who are awarded merit pay at least once in their first 3 years of service?
9. Is it possible that a good teacher could not receive merit pay but still be judged effective by students and parents?
10. Why is it that some teachers prefer working on a uniform pay scale?

7

TEACHER UNIONS
AND COLLECTIVE BARGAINING:
WHAT ARE YOUR VIEWS?

Teacher unions are a powerhouse force to be dealt with by all involved in education. In the United States, there are two major teacher unions. The National Education Association (NEA) is the older, more established, and larger of the two. The American Federation of Teachers (AFT), formally affiliated with organized labor (AFL-CLO), is concentrated in many large cities and surrounding suburbs around the country, but it is particularly strong in the Northeast. Once, these organizations had diametrically opposite goals. The NEA opposed collective bargaining, as they saw themselves as an organization of "professionals." The AFT campaigned vigorously for collective bargaining. Today, both organizations support collective bargaining, are politically active, and have advocates in key areas of government at all levels. They also have serious critics who claim that these two teacher organizations are roadblocks to educational innovation and progress.

Before we address that issue, we thought it would be beneficial to explore the origins and history of these teacher organizations. Most new teachers, and even many experienced ones, have very little knowledge of how, when, and why teacher unions came into existence. They are certainly unaware of the fact that the considerable power achieved by these two organizations is a relatively recent phenomenon. Yet today, much of a teacher's working conditions are governed by contractual obligations that can be found in the collective bargaining contract between the teacher organization and the school district in which that teacher may be employed. The teacher organizations themselves are often responsible for keeping teachers in the dark about what they have and have not accomplished for their membership. For example, many teachers believe that their collective bargaining contract ensures that tenure is available to them. This is absolutely false! Tenure preceded any collective bargaining agreement.

Most teachers are also unaware that collective bargaining did not exist until the United Federation of Teachers (UFT), the New York City local of the AFT, negotiated a contract with the New York City Board of Education, which was then approved by Mayor Robert Wagner in April 1961. From that historic agreement, teacher unionism spread rapidly to many of the large urban areas of America, and then spilled over into their suburbs.

The NEA was founded in 1857 and, for over 100 years, it could be characterized as a conservative, professional association. They were totally opposed to even the concept of collective bargaining and teacher strikes. As self-characterized professionals, they were fond of pointing out that attorneys did not strike and that physicians did not strike. Certainly, the NEA favored higher salaries, but it had absolutely no teeth with which to make these requests a reality. It was an organization that was heavily dependent on membership working in rural schools throughout the country, dominated by supervisors, be they superintendents or principals, and was often seen as devoid of a social conscience. This is best illustrated by the NEA's stand on the issue of civil rights and segregation. Even into the 1950s, the NEA continued to operate segregated chapters for local affiliates in many Southern cities and towns. Within the same city or town, there would be both a black chapter and a white chapter of NEA local. Yet, its considerable membership and lack of militancy made the NEA the organization commonly accepted by the general public and politicians as speaking for teachers, regardless of how effective it may have been.

The AFT was founded in 1916. It had a definite labor orientation and for many years was part of the AFL-CIO. Thus, its goal was to achieve formal collective bargaining agreements with school districts, similar to the goal of labor unions in the private sector. Although AFT membership was initially limited to virtually only three cities—Chicago, Washington, D.C., and New York City—these AFT affiliates were more militant than those of the NEA. These three cities contained the two largest school systems in the United States, and the total number of teachers employed made these cities very attractive for advocates of collective bargaining. It also should not be forgotten that the politicians of these cities tended to be pro labor.

The Great Depression of the 1930s was a period of some advances but even more setbacks for the AFT. Certainly the Great Depression elevated the status of teachers and dampened comparisons with "blue-collar" workers. Teaching was viewed as a privileged occupation. After all, teachers still had their "white-collar" jobs. They earned a regular paycheck, although their salaries were often reduced by mayors and boards of education because of the economic conditions of the time. The American public of that day viewed male teachers as being stable bread winners, bright, and devoted to children and as people who, in more positive economic times, might have been doctors or lawyers rather than teachers. Female teachers were viewed in much the same way, but with a few significant differences. If a female teacher was married, she was seen as simply supplementing her husband's income, so she didn't need a high salary. If she was single, whatever she earned would still enable her to spend her summer vacations traveling around the United States or Europe.

In answer to the question as to whether teacher unions are positive or negative influences in the world of education today, the authors are of two minds. We believe that when teacher unions negotiated collective bargaining contracts in the 1960s, they were of tremendous importance in trying to attract quality teachers into their school systems and in improving instruction, and, in general, were forces for positive change. We have lived long enough to now believe that our initial views were correct. We also believe, however, that teacher organizations have become rigid, bureaucratic relics whose main goal is to keep control of the leadership positions and perpetuate the goals of the organization rather than to improve education or to improve the daily lives of their member teachers.

These views are not only based on our observations from our "ivory tower" on what has gone on nationally in the past 50-plus years but also through out own experiences as young public school teachers. Two of the coauthors of this book were very active in their teacher union while serving as teachers in New York City. Obviously, we were at a very early stage of our professional lives at that time. We were idealistic, imbued with romantic notions about the goodness of unionism, as romanticized in tales of the Molly McGuires, and the forcefulness of such labor leaders as Walter Reuther, head of the United Auto Workers (UAW) and John L. Lewis of the United Mine Workers (UMW), as well as the writings and speeches of Norman Thomas, the many-time Socialist Party candidate for president of the United States. Our views were also shaped by the fact that all of us had fathers who were poor laborers who earned a few dollars at the end of the day. When our fathers returned home from their labors, we saw loved ones who appeared to be much older than they actually were. They were bent and misshapen long before they should have been. Thus, the three of us had a natural predilection toward teacher unionism from the very first day we walked into a school building. One of us (Marcus) became UFT chairperson in his school in 1959, three weeks after beginning his teaching career at a junior high school in the South Bronx. When he started working at the school in February 1959, he immediately joined the union, becoming the fourth UFT member. At that time, there was no collective bargaining contract, and union dues were $2 a month and collected monthly by the chapter chairperson, who then would forward whatever was collected to the union headquarters.

Marcus became chair during the third week of his teaching career. While teaching a class, the chapter chairperson walked into Marcus' room and congratulated him. When Marcus asked why he was receiving congratulations, he was told that the three other UFT members in the school had elected him to be the new chapter chairperson. At that time, there was neither monetary remuneration nor compensatory time for serving as chapter chairperson, and the previous chairperson simply did not want the job any longer. Not only was Marcus the chapter chairperson but, shortly thereafter, he was also given an entire New York City school district to oversee for the UFT, a district that contained 30-some schools. The UFT assigned a district leader to each school district with the goal of increasing membership in that district and to creating a sense of militancy and cohesion in the event that the push for collective bargaining resulted in a strike.

The point of this story is to let present-day teachers know that the teacher's union to which they may belong was not always that smooth, well-financed operation with offices and a bureaucracy that can rival that of the educational system employing teachers. Today, many local union chapters are almost totally out of touch with the aspirations, desires, feelings, and needs of their rank-and-file members. As UFT chapter chair in 1959, it was the job of the union chairperson to collect the $2 monthly dues from the handful of members in the school. Non-UFT members did not have to pay dues. One did not have to be a genius to understand that the health of the teacher union movement depended heavily on increasing its membership, and this became the highest priority. Collecting dues, even from the few union members, was no easy matter. To say the system was unwieldy would be an understatement. Looking back for us, or even for a new teacher reading this chapter, such a description would seem to belong in the Stone Age. Yet that's the way it was.

The post–World War II world had seen the United States emerge not only as one of the two most dominant military powers in the world but also as the world's economic colossus. As the post–World War II economy boomed, teaching as a career lost a good deal of the attractiveness that it had experienced during the Great Depression of the 1930s. The GI Bill of Rights after Word War II had resulted in many veterans being able to attend college, and a good number of those individuals were still attracted to teaching because their experiences as children in the 1930s had left many of them with the indelible view that civil service and job security would insulate them from the next Great Depression when it came.

This GI Bill resulted in a serious reshaping of the demographics of the teaching profession. More men now entered the field. The demographics of the nation's population were also changing due to the so-called baby boom that followed the end of World War II. No longer did marriages and having children need to be put off. The war was finally over, and normal life could resume. Thus, the teaching profession began to attract more male teachers at a time when there was an explosion of enrollments in our nation's schools. This increase in the school population was also compounded through increased immigration, particularly from Mexico and Puerto Rico.

The post–World War II era also saw a growth in demand for private homes that was closely correlated to the growth and demand for automobiles, which, in turn, was closely tied to the construction of highways leading into and out of our cities. The pent-up demand for autos, homes, appliances, furniture, and many other goods once considered luxury items resulted in the American economy moving from a wartime basis to a peacetime basis without missing a step. When the Cold War began in the late 1940s, the defense industries also benefited mightily. The American economy was booming.

The late 1940s and 1950s saw the purchasing power of teachers around the country decline. Many Americans saw a trade-off in becoming a teacher. One got a steady job with good daily hours, lots of holidays, and an 8- to 10-week summer vacation in return for modest pay that seemed to become more modest with the passing of each year.

One of the consequences of the economic boom was that schools became more crowded, and a tremendous teacher shortage developed. Teaching had always been a demanding profession, but the general public still had some distorted stereotypes of what teachers did and the compensation they received for doing it. Many Americans thought of teaching as women's work. The stereotypes of female teachers continued: If she was married, she was simply supplementing her husband's income; if she was single, she was economically well off and could afford to take numerous vacations during all of the time off that teachers enjoyed. There was a prevailing view among many parents that teachers magically appeared in the school building at 8:30 in the morning and disappeared at 3:00 in the afternoon.

This naïve view was deeply rooted. Most people did not understand that teachers had their own personal lives and did not suddenly appear between the hours of 8:30 A.M. and 3:00 P.M. to meet all of the needs of all of their children. Teachers needed to pay the rent, buy food and clothing, and deal with all of the ups and downs that life brings to us all.

There was also a view that the people attracted to teaching were not very strong willed. Had not Teddy Roosevelt stated that "Those who can, do, while those who can't, teach"? Simply stated, most of the general public thought of teachers as marshmallows who worked a half a day over a 10-month period with lots of time off within those 10 months. Given such views, combined with the economic boom in the private sector, teacher salaries stagnated. This, coupled with the increase in the school population, resulted in a serious shortage of teachers, particularly in the urban schools of America, at a time when the racial composition of those school systems was undergoing a serious transformation. Urban parents were taking their children into the suburbs. These children were being replaced by Latino and African American children of parents seeking greater social, political, and economic opportunities in our urban centers. These aspirations were similar to those of parents and grandparents of the children who were now leaving these same urban schools.

Thus, by the late 1950s and early 1960s, teaching as a career was becoming increasingly male but not in sufficient numbers to avoid a tremendous teacher shortage in schools located in the minority areas of cities in this country. This change greatly expedited the ability of the AFT in its struggle to achieve collective bargaining privileges for teachers. Many male teachers had young families, wives who stayed home to raise children and, as the only income producer, these teachers were forced to hold down second and even third jobs in order to earn enough money to support their families. Such individuals were more prone to accept the message put out by the AFT affiliates that collective bargaining would lead to better salaries and better working conditions and enhance learning opportunities for their children.

The shortage of teachers was particularly acute in those urban schools populated by the growing numbers of black and Latino children. It was not unusual for some classes at the secondary school level to go without a teacher for an entire academic year. Mondays and Fridays were particularly difficult days, as absenteeism among teachers increased noticeably on those days. Since few substitutes would venture into urban schools in big cities, it was not uncommon to put all of the uncovered classes into the auditorium, where cartoons or movies were shown, or to divide the uncovered classes into those classes that had teachers.

Without a collective bargaining process, administrators often thought of themselves as royalty. It sometimes seemed that they expected teachers to bow down three times as they passed them in the halls. The power of the principal was absolute and usually unquestioned. The school was almost regarded as the personal fiefdom of the principal—and heaven help those teachers who might question such an authority figure!

Even in the late 1950s, collective bargaining for public employees was still a dream, not a reality. As a matter of fact, the NEA actually opposed collective bargaining. The NEA was primarily rural based, while the AFT was primarily urban, limited mostly part to Washington, D.C., Chicago, and New York. The NEA was supervisor dominated, while the AFT was run by teachers. The NEA, at this time, was still operating segregated locals, while the AFT was in the forefront of the fight for black equality. In the 1960s, the AFT would become one of the prime financial supporters for Dr. Martin Luther King Jr. and his movement. The NEA believed that teachers were professionals and that professionals did not join labor unions. The AFT based its platform on economic and social issues, while addressing the issues of low salaries and inadequate employment conditions.

The notion that public employees could have collective bargaining rights was beyond the realm of imagination for much of the general public. After all, if teachers could get collective bargaining, then how could it not be granted to policeman, fireman, sanitation workers, and other civil service employees? Strikes in the private sector were not uncommon in this era, although much of the general public didn't believe teachers had the backbone of autoworkers, steelworkers, and coal miners. Teachers were largely regarded as milk-toasts. It was in this climate that the UFT undertook the big push to gain collective bargaining rights, a successful effort that would have huge consequences for public employees across the country.

The first step was to convince the mayor of New York City, Robert Wagner Jr., whose father had cosponsored the Wagner-Connery Act in 1935, which had amounted to an Emancipation Proclamation for union members, that teachers should have the right to unionize and to negotiate a collective bargaining contract. This was accomplished when Wagner agreed to an election to let teachers decide if, indeed, they wanted collective bargaining and to be represented by a union.

In 1959, the NEA did not even have an office in New York City. Initially, it had urged teachers to oppose the right to have collective bargaining. When teachers voted to have collective bargaining, and the actual selection of one was on the horizon, the NEA created something called the Teacher Bargaining Organization (TBO) to vie with the UFT to represent New York City teachers. The reputation of the NEA among most New York City teachers was so poor that it could not even resort to using the NEA initials—thus, the TBO took the field.

Surprisingly to many, the UFT won an overwhelming majority of the votes and emerged as the clear-cut winner to represent New York City teachers. Negotiations, however, were slow and not much was accomplished until a 1-day work strike in April of 1961 resulted in the City of New York negotiating a collective bargaining contract with the UFT, the first of its kind in the country. It was both a stirring victory and a surprising one.

This collective bargaining contract for civil service employees in a large city was a historic event that quickly had ramifications throughout the country for other municipal employees. In a short time, other municipal employees demanded and received the same right that the UFT had won for its members. Today, most new teachers have no idea when they begin their teaching careers how relatively recent and how difficult it was to achieve collective bargaining.

Many teachers and parents, particularly minority parents, initially believed that collective bargaining for teachers would lead to better schools. During the two 1-day strikes that had occurred, they carried signs reading: "Teacher Unions Mean Better Schools," "Better Salaries Mean Better Schools." Looking back, as naïve as it may have been, both the striking teachers and the supportive parents actually believed in the content of those signs.

By 1967, the UFT wanted to be involved in school improvement efforts and did so by pushing the concept of More Effective Schools (MES). This was the union's plan to try to reverse the decline in educational achievement in the lower socioeconomic areas of the city, populated largely by black and Puerto Rican youngsters. The MES program was predicated on smaller classes, more remedial instruction in math and reading, and more guidance counselors. The New York City Board of Education rejected these calls, claiming they did not have the money to implement MES throughout the city. The UFT was now bargaining for more than salaries and benefits. It considered involvement in the curriculum and the structuring of schools important enough to call a strike at the beginning of the 1967 school year. This strike lasted 14 working days, quite a drastic change from the single-day strikes of the two previous work stoppages. Eventually a compromise was reached, and the teachers returned to work.

The 14-day strike was a portent of things to come in the near future. During this strike, minority parents no longer supported teachers and, in schools in higher socioeconomic areas, teachers were now meaning-ful participants in the strike. This strike would have an enormous im-pact on teacher unions throughout the country. Municipal government, minority parents, community activists, and the business, cultural, and political leaders of New York City were, for the most part, aligned against the UFT. A change had also taken place in the politics of the city. John Lindsay, a photogenic, liberal Republican, had become mayor of New York City in 1965. Lindsay and Albert Shanker, now president of the UFT, had a strong personal antipathy toward one an-other. These negative personal feelings would have ramifications on the events that followed.

After the fall 1967 strike had ended, the Ford Foundation issued a re-port on the condition of New York City schools and how they could be improved. It was called the "Bundy Report," because McGeorge Bundy, president of the Ford Foundation, had considerable name recognition with the general public, based on his having served as a close advisor to Presidents Kennedy and Johnson. The Bundy Report stated that urban schools were failing minority students and that the situation could be improved only by "a reconnection of learning," something that could be achieved by giving parents a meaningful role in shaping and imple-menting educational policies in urban schools. To this end, the Bundy Report called for the decentralization of the highly centralized New York City school system, an action—if it occurred—that would have dis-persed educational power to various parent and community groups throughout the City of New York.

To prove that its plan could work, the Ford Foundation funded three demonstration school districts in the city. All three were located in neighborhoods in which the schools were largely attended by black and Puerto Rican children. These three demonstration districts received tremendous support in terms of favorable publicity from the *New York Times* and financial backing from the Ford Foundation. Very soon, militant activists, particularly from the black community, emerged, damning white teachers for being ineffective in teaching minority children. Some of these militants even accused teachers of being part of a conspiracy to purposely miseducate black children in order to "keep them down." These militants often seemed to use the words "white teachers" and "Jewish teachers" interchangeably. Given the city's large Jewish population, it was not surprising that many teachers were Jewish. The militants, however, simply seemed to assume that all teachers who were white were also Jewish. Similar situations developed shortly thereafter in Boston and Chicago, where teachers were heavily Irish Catholic, and in Newark, New Jersey, where teachers were heavily Italian. In all of these cities, there was tremendous racial tension.

As the situation got ugly, Shanker called for Lindsay to intervene and to condemn racial and religious bigotry, from whichever side it came. Lindsay turned a deaf ear, and the situation worsened. In the spring of 1968, the school board of the Ocean Hill-Brownsville, one of the three demonstration districts, terminated 18 tenured teachers. At first, no reasons were given for their termination. Under pressure, however, the school board simply declared that the teachers who had been terminated were philosophically out of tune with the goals of the district. Shanker warned Lindsay and the board of education that if due process was not followed, a citywide strike would be called. The UFT urged the terminated teachers to return to work. In the face of threats and worse, most did so. To the dismay of many citizens, viewers of the local news were treated nightly to these teachers returning to their schools every morning under a police escort while being subjected to a barrage of ugly racial and religious epitaphs. At times, they were even the targets of objects thrown at them. It was not pretty, but mercifully, the school year ended.

Over the summer, the issue was not resolved. Shanker had promised that city schools would not reopen in September without a solution, and he made good on that promise. From the first day of school in September into November 1968, the overwhelming number of New York City teachers went on strike. It was a strike that had many ramifications, some of them personal, others with great organizational impact. After the strike concluded, many teachers went for years without speaking to one another based on whether they had or had not participated in the strike. Albert Shanker and Rhody McCoy, head of the Ocean Hill-Brownsville school district, became national figures, as best evidenced by cover stories on them in *Time*. After the *Time* story, McCoy was invited to speak about the strike throughout the country. The strike had created an open rupture between organized teachers and minority parents. The issues involved in this strike were no longer local. Rather, they involved issues that could be found in every large city in America and even in some surrounding suburbs.

The issues on which this strike was based were complex. Certainly, the UFT's concern about the total denial of due process to its teachers was an important item. What gave the strike such national prominence, however, were other issues. By 1968, the populations of most urban school districts had already become or were rapidly becoming majority black or Hispanic. The professional staff responsible for educating these youngsters remained heavily white. As test scores plummeted, the dropout rate soared, and violence in schools became more prevalent, many black leaders placed the blame squarely on white teachers and administrators. They maintained that most white educators did not care about their students, did not believe they were capable of learning, and, as mentioned earlier, were even purposely miseducating black students in order to keep them in a subordinate position in society. Among New York City educators, a fair number of teachers were of Puerto Rican descent, particularly in those schools with large numbers of Puerto Rican youngsters. This group tended to be divided over their support of the strike. Many struck, while many others did not.

It was frightening for many white teachers to watch the evening news and see the anger and, in some cases, hatred voiced by black parents and activists directed toward them. One result of this, however, that was beneficial to the UFT was that membership rolls skyrocketed. No longer was it difficult for chapter chairs to enroll passive teachers. After watching the evening news the previous night, the next morning many teachers sought out their UFT chapter chair to sign their membership card.

Certainly many of the criticisms of urban schools were valid. There was a paucity of minority teachers and almost a total absence of minority administrators. The three demonstration districts, however, were headed by minority superintendents and most of the principals were also minority. In the late 1960s, it was also not difficult to attract idealistic, young whites into the ranks of the teaching staffs of those demonstration districts and even to other city schools. The Vietnam War was raging, and teachers could receive draft deferments for working in inner-city schools. Many college campuses were cauldrons of antiwar and pro–civil rights activities. Thus, there was no shortage of white sympathizers supporting Lindsay, the Ford Foundation, and the cultural, business, and political establishment of the city.

The strike ended with no side fully satisfied. There was a tacit understanding of a need for more minority teachers and administrators. The Ford Foundation had already funded programs, such as the one at Fordham University, aimed at producing minority administrators for urban school districts. The changing demography of the school population was inexorable. The school system populations around the country became more heavily minority, but the notion that more minority teachers would automatically result in minority children learning more never materialized. Looking back, it seems almost naïve that many people once actually believed that the solution to the problem of low achievement among minority youths was to employ more black educators. If only life were so simple!

The events preceding, during, and following the "Great Strike" of 1968 had immense impact on future policies of teacher unions around the country. Whereas teacher unions had once seen collective bargaining as the "pot of gold" at the end of the rainbow, the Great Strike taught them otherwise. They realized that vocal and powerful groups were working to erode hard-earned gains achieved over decades of effort. The UFT and other affiliates around the country now went into a "circle the wagon" mentality. The organization would now need to grow larger and become much more politically active. It would expand activities in various state capitals to ensure that favorable legislation was passed and unfavorable legislation was either rejected or watered down.

It is debatable whether the NEA and AFT would have evolved as they have to this day if the Great Strike of 1968 had not occurred. The AFT was stunned by the events and criticisms made of it and its members by minority group members in 1967 and 1968, given their past history of support for black and minority equality. What is not debatable, however, is that teacher unions now gave priority to the aims of the organization and not the aims of its members.

In the 1970s, the NEA lobbied effectively for the creation of a separate Department of Education in Washington, D.C. and, because of its early support of Jimmy Carter for the presidential nomination, this became a reality upon his election. Teacher organizations won the right to have every teacher covered by a collective bargaining contract and to have their union membership dues automatically deducted from their paychecks, whether or not they wanted to join the union. Teacher union support of victorious political candidates brought with it widespread political influence. At times, however, individual union members came to resent that their dues were being expended on behalf of candidates they opposed. This has resulted in court cases, many of them quite current, focusing on the legality of how the teacher unions used membership dues. In the spring of 2007, the U.S. Supreme Court will issue a decision involving the legality of the use of fees paid to an NEA local in the state of Washington by those who choose not to join a union but who must nevertheless pay union dues, called an *agency fee.*

Without question, Albert Shanker became the most prominent spokesman for organized teachers after the Great Strike of 1968. To his credit, he had evolved from a union leader into an educational statesman by the time of his death in 1997. Shanker was a great proponent of public education, of which he was a product. He also understood that, if educators were not flexible in accepting positive, meaningful change, then public schooling as it existed in the United States would cease to exist. He was not an automatic opponent of change. Rather, he questioned whether change, without supporting research data, would lead to greater student achievement. He came to accept the need for looking at the way teachers were compensated and became an advocate for a form of merit pay. He was a workaholic who was as well versed in every aspect of what was taking place educationally in this country as any education professor or other so-called expert. He was a tireless worker on behalf of better schools for children. His elevation to the presidency of the AFT gave him a national platform, best illustrated by his weekly paid advertisement column in the Sunday *New York Times,* which became a must-read for most "shakers" and "doers" in politics and education.

Regrettably, Shanker's passing from the scene created a void in the teacher union movement that has yet to be filled. The NEA has had some strong leaders in the past 30 years, but it too seems to be out of touch with its membership in the schools. Criticisms that teacher unions are automatic enemies of reform are probably overdone. On the other hand, both the NEA and AFT are gigantic influences in the politics and pedagogy of education. One of the major critics of teacher unions, Myron Lieberman, a former candidate for the presidency of the AFT, has pointed out that the growth of both teacher organizations has been phenomenal and has occurred at a time when union membership in other sectors of the economy has dramatically declined. Instead of being in the vanguard of advocating positive reform of our schools, however, the two teacher organizations have been staunch opponents of giving greater school choice to parents and their children. Both teacher unions are caught in a situation where they are worried about protecting organizational gains rather than improving our nation's public schools. Both unions have similar policies and objectives and, at various times, locals of these two unions have merged at the state level. There have been times when it seemed that a merger at the national level was imminent, but it has yet to occur.

In the past two decades, many of the over three million members of the NEA and AFT have grown more distant and alienated from their organization as conditions in schools have worsened. Yet, change of leadership in various locals has been hard to bring about. For example, the Unity Caucus of the UFT has been in continuous power since the organization came into existence. Visits to various New York City schools, particularly to secondary schools, indicate a deep dissatisfaction with the leadership of UFT.

We still believe in the right of teachers to bargain collectively. The three of us remember well what it was like to teach prior to collective bargaining. We can assure the reader that life was neither simpler nor better prior to collective bargaining. Our disappointment with teacher unions is that we believe their promises and potential for improving schools have been largely unfulfilled. As young participants in two teacher strikes, we believed that collective bargaining for teachers would improve the quality of schools. We believe that many of the major figures who fought for collective bargaining would also be disappointed with the results. Little evidence suggests that there is a teacher union leader on the horizon who can lead a move for significant change in the positions of either the NEA or AFT. On the other hand, many commentators said the same thing in 1932, in the midst of the Great Depression. Perhaps there is an educational statesman who will emerge, as did Franklin Delano Roosevelt in an earlier time of crisis.

KEY QUESTIONS FOR TEACHERS

1. How would teachers fare today if there were no teacher unions?
2. What, if anything, have teacher unions done for students?
3. Have teacher unions helped or hindered teaching from becoming a profession?
4. Have teacher unions helped raise the standards of teaching?
5. To what extent have teacher unions influenced instruction in the classroom?
6. In what ways has collective bargaining improved the manner in which teachers have been treated?
7. Should teacher unions be involved in the offering of in-service courses for teachers?
8. Should unions be concerned about merit pay for teachers?
9. Do unions assist individual teachers as much as they assist groups of teachers?
10. Can teaching as a true profession be reconciled with collective bargaining rights for teachers?

8

TEACHING PERFORMANCE
AND ACCOUNTABILITY:
PROBLEMS OR OPPORTUNITIES?

Teaching performance and accountability has raised a great deal of harsh dialogue and, indeed, unanticipated confrontation among teachers, administration, school boards, state legislators, higher education institutions, and the taxpaying public. Why would this subject evoke such an emotional outburst and be challenged by so many organizations?

It is regrettable that when the issue of the low quality of our nation's schools is raised by the media, various state legislatures, and school boards, blame is usually directed at the classroom teacher. This is followed by an outcry for improved teacher performance and greater accountability. Those who point that finger fail to recognize that accountability and teacher performance are a product of those:

- who prepare teachers at higher education institutions and set the admission criteria to teacher education programs
- school districts and school leaders who provide in-service training, select the teachers, award tenure, and are responsible for setting promotional policies, academic standards, and a host of other actions that have an impact on teacher performance
- who prepare the budgets of the respective districts that determine class size, teacher workloads, tutorial services, and salaries

- who prepare the tax base of the district, and the legislators who establish the state minimum foundation programs for all districts that determine the ability of the respective districts to allocate the necessary funds to attract outstanding teachers and retain them.

Accountability and the classroom performance of students do not rest solely on the competence of the classroom teacher. Performance evaluation must be a comprehensive, top-to-bottom process involving all the educational and political institutions and those functionaries in the business of education. In 2006, the National Education Association (NEA) announced that the organization will accept teacher accountability measures as proposed by the No Child Left Behind (NCLB) legislation, but that reforms in the NCLB Act were needed. They did, however, emphasize that those who are the decision makers in controlling the financing of schools also should be held accountable. Reg Weaver, president of the NEA, pointed out that both parties must accept responsibility and be held accountable for failing schools. Adequate funding must be provided in reducing class size and rethinking the rigid requirements and guidelines that threaten teachers' positions. Funds must be made available to provide educational services to students in need of specialized help.

The NEA's Representative Assembly argued that there were flaws in the NCLB Act that needed to be corrected. The NEA expressed its desire to move away from depending solely on testing and to consider the abilities and circumstances of students as part of the total profile.

The authors are concerned that such considerations as the economic status of the student's family and the total makeup of the given school population are being ignored in the NCLB Act. Research clearly demonstrates that test scores correlate with economic and social class. Test scores are consistently lower in economically disadvantaged communities.

Would educational results of bright, highly achieving and motivated students attending the prestigious Bronx High School of Science or Stuyvesant High School in New York City change much if the faculties of these two schools were exchanged with the faculties of two central-city urban high schools? Further, would such an exchange of faculties result in greater student learning and accomplishment in the two inner-city high schools as a result of being exposed to teachers with proven track records of success? The authors are not certain as to what would happen in such a circumstance. We are inclined to agree with the findings of the Illinois study that found that good teachers make a great difference in the education process of disadvantaged students. On the other hand, student achievement in the inner-city schools would not approximate the achievement of students in Science or Stuyvesant high schools. We also believe that the students in these two special schools for the academically gifted would continue to do well regardless of who was teaching them.

Premier high schools like those cited usually have fully certified teachers with considerable successful classroom experience. Central-city schools and those in poorer districts usually are staffed with beginning teachers and those who are not fully certified in their teaching fields or are teaching out of license. Also, one has to remember that those premier high schools in New York City have a student population that consists of the top students, and they are more motivated to be active participants in the learning and teaching process. It is very difficult to single out poor or outstanding teachers without examining all the factors that contribute to the success and failure of all the forces at play in learning and teaching.

The authors readily admit that there are incompetent teachers who should be terminated but, because they are tenured, are unlikely to be removed from their positions because of the legal and due process protections afforded teachers. There are also beginning teachers who really are not ready to handle a classroom assignment. Yet, who is to be held accountable for such teachers being in the classroom? Do we ever ask for the superintendent's resignation for poor teacher performance? Not usually. When superintendents are terminated, as they often are, it is usually because of factors far removed from the classroom performance of teachers in their districts—yet it is the superintendent who should be the first one to be held accountable, along with the university or college staff who prepared these incompetent teachers and gave them their stamp of approval. It is interesting to note that school administrators prepare the vast majority of teacher performance evaluation reports. Most school systems do not subscribe to the policy of giving considerable weight to peer review in probationary and tenure decisions. Unlike universities and colleges, where peer review is a very dominant factor in the decision-making process, K–12 procedures often give either lip service or minimal weight to peer review. Furthermore, teachers are seldom invited to contribute to the evaluation criteria that are to be used to judge their performance.

The authors do not wish to convey the impression that accountability should not be applied to the classroom teacher. However, we need to look at the broader perspective rather than just addressing accountability for classroom teachers. We are being dragged into a conflict that cannot be resolved piecemeal unless we address all the issues surrounding this problem.

Let us review some of these issues:

- How are teachers prepared?
- What kind of support do teachers receive when they enter the profession?
- Are these entering teachers at or near being top students in their college graduating classes, as measured by their GPAs?
- Are the teachers fully certified, or do they hold temporary or substitute teaching licenses or certification when they are hired by school districts?
- What objective criteria are used to evaluate teacher success?

There really is no reason for teacher performance and accountability to be so volatile if we systematically review *all* the parties who are accountable for the successful operation of our schools, rather than begin this process simply by focusing primarily on the classroom teacher.

Teachers need to be given leadership opportunities to develop new approaches to accountability. Teacher leadership councils should be established at every school. Teachers, not administrators, must police their profession and take action if any of their colleagues fail to demonstrate professional improvement or are judged as not meeting even the minimal expectations of the profession. Teachers are the best judges of professional competence if unfettered by union "politics."

The model of the future should include teacher mentors who, because of their teaching expertise, are qualified to provide peer assistance and to make judgments about their colleagues' teaching performances. It seems that teachers are more likely to accept recommendations and intervention by a mentor teacher rather than from an administrator who may have been away from actual teaching for years, perhaps even decades. It is our experience that many teachers do not view administrators favorably. The salaries of teacher mentors should be comparable to that of key administrators. They should be given special recognition and be assigned a crucial role in upgrading teacher performance.

The numerous federal and state mandates being implemented to measure accountability and performance all fail to address the major problems facing the profession:

- Inadequate salaries
- Low admission standards into the profession
- Weak professional teacher training programs
- Discipline and safety issues
- Mediocre teacher preparation programs sponsored by many colleges

Many of the problems associated with performance and accountability would be alleviated if the teaching profession could attract outstanding students who are majoring in the sciences, humanities, mathematics, computer science, and executive business programs. Students considering becoming doctors, research scientists, engineers, and corporate executives must be tempted to think of a career in education. Top students are needed to join the ranks of teachers.

Despite what has been stated in this chapter, we in the teaching profession cannot ignore critics such as Bill O'Reilly, the television personality and journalist, who sometimes asks questions that we should heed. In a recent column, he pointed out that *Newsweek* reported that American 15-year-olds ranked 15th worldwide in reading assessment, while the United States is spending the highest amount of money on education of all countries in the history of civilization. According to Mr. O'Reilly, money alone is not the only answer to a sound education. We agree! An excessive amount of attention has been directed at expenditures and very little on effective strategies to improve learning and teaching.

It has been suggested that accountability should start with the parents. Research has demonstrated that children whose parents are taking an active interest in their school performance are more likely to succeed in school.

KEY QUESTIONS FOR TEACHERS

1. How can more high-achieving undergraduate students be attracted into the teaching profession?
2. Should the preparation of teachers be in the hands of local school districts?
3. Why is it primarily teachers who are held accountable for the performance of their students?
4. Can good teachers succeed in educating all children, regardless of the abilities of those children?
5. What do you believe is a minimum job performance standard for successful teachers?
6. How could your college teacher preparation program be improved?
7. Every profession has competent as well as incompetent practitioners. How can the teaching profession rid itself of incompetent teachers?
8. Evaluation of a teacher's work is up to the supervisors. If a school fails to adequately educate children, and no teacher in that school is judged to be incompetent, who is accountable?
9. Is the amount of money spent on education a criterion of a good school?

9

MOBILITY IN THE PROFESSION: POLITICS OR MERIT?

Mobility in the profession once meant, "How do I get out of my class-room teaching position into an easier, higher paying job?" This was probably always an oversimplification. Today, education is a lot more complex, and this axiom now has many twists and turns to it. The authors still maintain that the classroom teacher has the most difficult job to perform in the delivery of educational services. Teachers might now enjoy duty-free lunch periods and some professional preparation time during the day, but the actual instructional process is the most relentless and exhausting activity that goes on in the school. When a teacher is assigned to a specific room at a specific time with a specific class, regardless of mood, he or she must be there, ready to deliver instruction to the best of his or her abilities.

As young teachers, we quickly realized how difficult our job was. We also looked around us and saw certain individuals and asked what it was that they did. They usually carried titles like guidance counselor, assistant principal, or even principal. All of these positions paid more than a teacher's wages, even those teachers at or near maximum on the pay scale. It also seemed to us that they had much more flexibility in terms of how they spent their time. They did not have to meet a difficult class the last period of the day on a Friday afternoon. It seemed to us that if pressures on them reached a certain point, they simply could, and sometimes did, walk around the block in order to reduce stress. The classroom teacher never had that luxury. He or she had to be wherever his or her teaching schedule told him or her to be. We were not the only ones who sized up the educational structure in this way. This was best exemplified by the enormous number of teachers who sought to get out of the classroom for what they considered to be greener pastures.

Mobility in the education profession usually meant getting out of the classroom and serving in some other capacity. By saying this, we do not mean to infer that *any* job in education is an easy one. As a matter of fact, the many professionals who do nonclassroom–teaching jobs are under enormous pressures, comparable to those confronting the classroom teacher. We still maintain, however, that although the jobs may not be easy ones, they are less arduous than being a classroom teacher. However, in the 21st century, we are witnessing a situation in which many classroom teachers are no longer interested in positions such as assistant principal, principal, and superintendent.

In many school districts in the United States, teachers are now adequately paid. In New York City and the surrounding suburbs, for example, teachers can earn $100,000+ annually on maximum pay. They work approximately 180 days per year, enjoy the privilege of tenure, and can supplement their salaries by working various extracurricular jobs such as coaching or directing after-school clubs. Virtually all school administrators must work an 11-month work year, and they often start their new position at a salary lower than what they earned as a teacher. In addition, when they move from classroom teacher into a counseling or administrative position, be it in the same district or not, they give up their tenure. Of course, they may earn tenure as counselor, assistant principal, or principal—but they must earn that tenure for their performance in their new position.

Perhaps most critical to the change in the mobility system in education is the fact that building- and district-level administrators are now under greater parental, community, and governmental pressures than has ever been the case before. Not only must administrators work an 11-month year, but their days usually do not conclude at the same time as the days of the teachers they supervise. Many young teachers now look at their building and district administrators and conclude that it is no longer worth it to aspire for their positions. This view accounts for the considerable dip in the talent pool of teachers looking to move into the field of school administration. We are not saying that talented teachers are not striving to become administrators; we are saying that *fewer* talented teachers are seeking to become administrators.

From conversations with individuals who run search firms, we have been told that the pool of candidates seeking superintendencies is down dramatically. Fifteen years ago, 75 to 90 candidates would apply for such a vacancy. Today, 15 to 20 candidates might apply for the same position. Search firms usually are asked to present anywhere from three to seven names to the board of education as finalists for a position. Individuals who would not have made such a final list 15 years ago now make the cut and are presented to the board of education. Although the superintendency has never been an easy job, we can say with certainty that it is getting even more difficult. Members of local boards of education often think that they know more than their superintendent on education issues and regularly not only inject themselves into the policy making aspect of running a district but also want to micromanage the implementation of those policies.

Parents, be they with children in inner-city schools or suburban schools, see education as the prime vehicle for their children to achieve vertical social mobility in our society. Thus, when children fail to perform up to the expectations of their parents, it is usually the school administrator who is asked why this is the case. Parents rarely look beyond the perceived failure of the school to adequately instruct their children to explain why they are not performing at a level of academic excellence.

We are also in an era when many big-city school systems are coming directly under the influence of their mayors. It seems as if the general public no longer has total trust in the educational establishment to adequately run school systems. Indeed, given test score results in many urban school systems, perhaps such a view is justified. After all, so goes the thinking, if the mayor of a city is in charge of the schools, at least he or she will be accountable for the performance of those schools on election day. In New York City, Los Angeles, Chicago, and other large cities, the mayors now select the chancellor or superintendent of the school system. There is no doubt, however, as to where ultimate responsibility is placed—it is with the mayors of those cities.

There has never been a perfect educational era. School systems have constantly moved from systems of organizations that were decentralized, then centralized, back to decentralized, and then recentralized. Many of these organizational changes are made to simply buy time so that the educators and politicians can claim that they are improving the quality of education. By the time these organizational changes have been shown not to have any dramatic educational impact on improving student learning, the educators and politicians responsible for the change have moved on, and the "game" can be restarted for a new generation of parents and children with little recall of the previous failures.

Great administrators, like great teachers, can make an extraordinary difference in the lives of the children, parents, and staff of a given school building or school district. Reality tells us that there are few great practitioners and leaders in any field. Education is no different. In order to make administration more attractive to teachers, salaries are increasing significantly. In thinking of the responsibilities of a superintendent, try comparing those responsibilities with those of the CEO of major company. Joel Klein, chancellor of the New York City school system, earns approximately $250,000 annually, plus perks. Rudy Crew, superintendent of the Miami-Dade County school system, earns $295,000 annually. Many citizens are dismayed that educators earn this kind of money. Our view is that this is convoluted thinking.

How much would a CEO in the private sector earn if he or she were running a company of over 100,000 employees, over one million product consumers (children seeking knowledge), and overseeing a budget of over $15 billion annually? The answer is not certain, but we do know that it would be a lot more than what Chancellor Klein earns for running the New York City school system. The public must get over the notion that educators should not be paid well for what they do. Many suburban school boards are realizing that, if they have a superintendent with whom they are satisfied, many other districts would like to hire away that individual. The result is that many school boards, in order to keep such a superintendent, are going to have to pay for that privilege. Thus, for example, in the New York City metropolitan area, it is no longer unusual for superintendents to earn between $200,000 and $250,000 per year, plus perks.

The shortage of outstanding school leaders has resulted in an interesting change of direction in education. Fifteen years ago, all school administrators would have come through the ranks of the education profession, with the first position held being that of teacher. Today, it is not unusual for district leaders to have no experience in the field of education prior to their appointment. We are seeing generals from the military, attorneys, business types, and even former politicians, such as Roy Romer, former governor of Colorado, running large school systems. The logic for this is based on the belief that bright, outstanding leaders who know how to get things done can run a school system, as this is just an organization like any other. No longer do we think of experience in education as a necessity for running an educational organization.

Usually, in cases where noneducators have been appointed to run school systems, that noneducator is intelligent enough to surround himself or herself with individuals who do have backgrounds in curriculum, testing, and a host of other areas of education. Have educational miracles been brought about where noneducators have led the educational system? Of course not! Many of these noneducators have brought new ideas with them. Regrettably, like the ideas of their educational predecessors, such ideas are also "doomed to success." For example, in New York City an effort to upgrade the quality of building principals resulted in the creation of a Leadership Academy. A small fortune has been spent on attracting and training principal candidates from all over the country. A corporate figure was brought in to oversee this Leadership Academy. He was available because the company for which he served as CEO went bankrupt. Despite glowing press reviews, most New York City regional superintendents only grudgingly accept graduates of the academy as principals in their district, and one superintendent refuses to accept any. This is based on the perceived quality and performance of initial graduates of the academy and their on-the-job performance.

Positions as building-level administrators still possess more of an attraction than a superintendency, yet even positions such as principal and assistant principal are now more pressure-packed than ever before. Many parents have unrealistic expectations of what a building administrator can achieve. Indeed, some building administrators are so talented that they can facilitate significant educational progress on the part of their staff and students. Most such principals do not gain this ability from the postgraduate programs that are preparing administrators. Some administrators just have a natural feel for what it takes to lead a school and everyone in it. Such individuals usually have considerable common sense, personal integrity, and tremendous enthusiasm, which they bring to their job on an everyday basis. Such leaders have great respect for the difficulties facing teachers in the instructional process. They also realize that they have their jobs because students attend their schools and that all education decisions must first consider what is in the best interest of those students.

The No Child Left Behind (NCLB) Act and many state mandates have put a crushing paperwork burden on building-level administrators. The outstanding building leader should be devoting much of his or her time to improving instruction in the school. Nothing else should take away from this vital task. Even before NCLB, however, some building leaders felt more comfortable taking care of administrative aspects of the position rather than with the instructional leadership component. Thus, the complaint that NCLB is getting in the way of instructional leadership is not always a valid one. We must admit, however, that even building leaders who recognize the primary importance of instructional leadership are now complaining that they must spend many hours after school doing all of the paperwork required of them and that the amount of time required for this onerous task is multiplying.

Many parents assume that the building leader is omnipotent and has the miraculous ability to have their children perform at or above grade standards. When reality sets in, considerable disappointment, frustration, and anger can be directed at the building leader. The failures of children are often attributed by parents to the failure of the building leader to function in an appropriate manner.

As with superintendents, salaries for building administrators have been increasing significantly because of the necessity to attract good people into those positions. As we said earlier, many teachers, when comparing their jobs with those of administrators at the building and district levels, come to the conclusion that they would rather stay where they are. There are, however, teachers who dislike what they do to such a great extent that no deterrent will keep them from trying to leave the classroom. Such individuals can earn certification as administrators, guidance counselors, or school psychologists. Other positions in a school that may not require certification include deans of behavior, lunch room coordinator, security coordinator, supply coordinator, and union representative. These positions usually require some amount of teaching during the school day but at a reduced level. We are not saying that everyone who aspires to leave the classroom is doing so because he or she hates being there, however. Many teachers think they can have greater impact and derive more personal satisfaction by functioning in another position. Yet we would be naïve if we did not point out that all individuals who seek to leave the classroom may not have a positive motive for doing so.

Some teachers are so desperate to leave the classroom that they will use political connections to do so. Recently, the *New York Times* carried a story about a teacher who was thought to be having sex with one of her teenage students and, when the principal tried to intervene, he discovered that the teacher in question had sufficient "pull" in the community to make disciplinary action an impossibility. Regrettably, we do not think that such cases are isolated situations. It is children who must be served, rather than educators who may be politically connected.

One of the contradictions of education is that oftentimes when one leaves the classroom, one might never again teach children. This is something that must change. The building-level administrator should function as the head teacher. Not only must the building leader have administrative skills, but he or she should also possess the ability to walk into a classroom and demonstrate to other teachers what a master lesson should look like. Building leaders should have at least one classroom assignment per day. There is a tremendous difference between *telling* a teacher how to improve instructional effectiveness and being able to walk into a classroom and actually *demonstrate* to other teachers how to improve instruction. At the college and university level, it is not unusual for deans to teach at least one class. Doing so is not only beneficial for the morale of other faculty, but it also gets that administrator away from behind his or her desk and all of the paperwork piled up on it. Teaching a class is also a good reminder to the administrator and the teaching staff that what goes on in the classroom is the most important activity that goes on in the school.

In order to keep teachers who love what they are doing in the classroom, we urge that outstanding teachers earn the same approximate salaries as their building administrators. If we accept the principle that classroom instruction is indeed the most important aspect of the school day, then we must recognize this on payday. Great teachers cannot be lost to the classroom forever because of a desire to earn more money as a building administrator. Great teachers who do not have a desire to be an administrator should not be penalized for remaining in the classroom.

What can we do to attract more good people into the field of administration? First of all, parents must have realistic expectations that very few, if any, miracles take place overnight in the world of education. Failing school systems do not suddenly turn on a dime and become paragons of excellence. Improvement is slow, but it is improvement that we are seeking. A number of years ago, one of us attended the installation of a new superintendent in a New York City school district. Sitting in the packed auditorium, it was striking what the incoming superintendent was promising parents in terms of the educational turnaround for the students in the district over the next 3 years. With each promise there was greater applause. After the ceremony, the superintendent and one of the authors went for a bite to eat. The author inquired how in the world the new superintendent would ever be able to deliver on what was promised earlier that evening. His response was very interesting. Of course, he realized that he could not deliver on his promises. He admitted that if he was fortunate enough to stay for 10 years as superintendent, he might begin to approach on the delivery of some of those promises. He then asked a question: "Do you think the school board would have selected me as superintendent if I told them I had a plan that would take 10 to 15 years to implement?" The answer to the question was obvious. The new superintendent was playing the educational game. The school board was playing the educational game. Politicians play the same educational game. Colossal success is right around the corner. What nonsense!

KEY QUESTIONS FOR TEACHERS

1. As a classroom teacher, do you enjoy what you are doing?
2. What would make it attractive for you to leave the classroom for another position in the educational structure?

3. Do you have recommendations for dealing with teachers who do not enjoy being in the classroom?

4. Do you believe that nonclassroom educators should earn more money than classroom teachers?

5. Do you believe that school district leaders are comparable to corporate CEOs and should be paid accordingly?

6. How can we eliminate political favoritism in the employment of out-of-classroom personnel?

7. How can we make the position of classroom teacher more attractive so that outstanding teachers do not feel they must leave that position in order to earn more money?

8. How can we make building- and district-level leadership positions more attractive in order to increase the pool of outstanding candidates for such positions?

9. How can we deal with parents who have unrealistic expectations as to what a building leader can accomplish for their children?

10. Do you believe that all professional educators in a school should teach at least one class? How can this be accomplished?

III

EFFECTIVE LEARNING
AND TEACHING

10

EFFECTIVE CLASSROOM MANAGEMENT: CAN IT BE ACHIEVED?

To be an effective leader, one must be a skilled manager. The teaching profession must recognize that, although learning and teaching methodologies are central to a teacher's basic professional preparation and success, effective classroom management skills are an essential prerequisite. Without an organized, functional classroom that includes clear, specific rules, regulations, procedures, and expectations, chaos will engulf a teacher's energies and learning will be compromised.

The quality of education our students receive is of paramount importance. If the quality of classroom instruction is going to be addressed, we must first come to grips with the issue of effective classroom management. How a teacher presents the rules, regulations, and expectations to the students should not only be articulated in clear language but in a tone that promotes a positive climate, not one of intimidation and fear. Students need to understand the consequences of breaking the rules and why rules and regulations are required for the common good. Schools should periodically distribute newsletters to parents and students to reinforce the school policies.

There are over 50 million students attending American schools in grades K–12. Given this vast number of students with different backgrounds, abilities, interests, and special needs, it is almost an impossible task and a monumental challenge to provide a classroom setting that will promote the best interests of each child. Yet the teacher must use every vehicle and strategy available to achieve an effective learning environment. Our schools must provide an organized classroom atmosphere:

- where each student feels safe
- where there is an environment conducive to learning and teaching
- where each student is respected
- where each student understands and clearly accepts responsibility and the consequences of his or her actions
- where the teacher is fair and patient, and provides good managerial judgment in the exercise of administering professional duties and responsibilities.

Teachers might not be classified as administrators but, in essence, they are perhaps the key administrators in the school since they actually administer the classrooms in the building.

It goes without saying that the teacher who is unable to control and maintain order in the classroom and who violates basic classroom management techniques is doomed to failure. That is why the authors have focused on this subject. The authors regret that teacher preparation programs do not place greater emphasis on this particular aspect of the professional skills required to be a successful teacher.

There are those who may deny the authors' assumption that the teacher's personality plays an important role in good classroom management, control, and discipline. Over the years, the authors have observed teachers walk into a class with an almost indefinable presence about them and immediately obtain the students' respect. Not a word needs to be said. It is how the teacher acts, speaks for himself or herself, and makes a silent statement to the students.

A teacher's smile, handshake, and encouraging words go a long way toward developing a warm, productive classroom atmosphere. Daily attendance is not only a legal requirement but lets the students know that they are being monitored. This helps the teacher become familiar with the students' names and identities.

Teachers should always remember that they are in control, but they need to exude positive, friendly energy. In addition, they should do everything humanly possible not to lose their poise, to avoid sarcasm, and to provide fair punishment. Teachers must acquire the skills necessary to be a good listener to student concerns. They should be alert at all times as to what transpires in the classroom. Teachers must encourage students and help them gain self-confidence.

The physical conditions in the classroom are very important. Cheerful bulletin boards, clean floors and blackboards, organized seating arrangements, neat desks, good ventilation, and adequate shade cover from the sun are all contributing factors to a pleasant classroom environment.

Classroom management responsibilities have become a more critical problem with the escalation of attacks by students on teachers, increased student aggression and bullying tactics toward fellow students, gang activities on the school premises, and the increase of sexual predators in a school building, included among them even teachers. The teacher must always be vigilant and concerned for student safety. Safety is now in the forefront of major concerns facing the educational establishment. Concerns about academic achievement are now surpassed by safety and disciplinary problems. Good classroom management is no guarantee that safety issues will be alleviated, but it is a necessary step that must be implemented and carefully observed.

Make no mistake that students are fully capable of understanding why rules are established and why everyone benefits from these regulations in the class. Teachers and parents need to be role models who present positive attitudes and encouragement to students to follow school rules. A poor classroom manager cannot be a successful teacher.

Teachers, especially beginning teachers, need to develop a classroom management checklist. This list will serve as a reminder as well as reinforce those organizational items needing the teacher's attention. The list should be periodically reviewed and refined, depending on classroom circumstances.

Teachers also need to organize a student file in which notations of student behavior as well as academically related issues can be recorded. Teachers need to recognize symptoms that should be brought to the attention of a school counselor or psychologist. For this reason, teachers should receive sensitivity training to develop the professional skills and competencies to recognize students with behavioral manifestations and special learning needs.

Research, as well as the recent Gallop polls, have pointed out that discipline and safety issues have been singled out as the most serious problems facing today's schools. The failure of so many students in achieving success has also raised grave concerns. J. S. Kounin pointed out almost four decades ago in his book *Discipline and Group Management in Classrooms* that there are successful and ineffective classroom management strategies and that each of them has an impact on elementary school children and their learning development.

This is not new information. Decades ago, Allan Ornstein and Daniel Levine in an article entitled "Teacher Behavior Research: Overview and Outlook," published in *Phi Delta Kappa*, singled out successful classroom managerial techniques as being vital to teacher performance and retention in the profession. These studies, plus those by numerous other investigators, reinforce the authors' position of the importance of classroom management skills. The authors submit the following specific recommendations to assist teachers with their classroom management:

- The classroom and bulletin boards must be attractive.
- Materials distributed to students must have educational value and be presented in an orderly fashion.
- Class procedures and regulations must be clearly explained to the students.
- Teachers should be well-dressed, use appropriate speech, and exhibit good hygiene.
- Avoid confrontational situations with students.
- Be polite and respectful.
- Welcome input from the students.
- Accountability for the behavior and academic performance of students needs to be consistently reinforced.
- Prepare lesson plans and units of study in advance.
- Flexibility must be applied in the learning process.
- Be sensitive to special symptoms indicating behavioral and learning problems.
- Become familiar with your students; know their names and interests.
- Promote self-confidence in each student.
- Treat all the students fairly, and be patient when problems arise.

- Utilize all the school's human resources, such as counselors and psychologists.
- Never use corporal punishment or physical force except when protecting the safety of other students.
- Take an active, not passive, interest in student activities and special concerns.
- When feasible, first attempt to handle classroom problems on your own before making a referral or involving the administration.
- Give thoughtful homework assignments; they should be grade, age, and content appropriate.
- Provide each student with opportunities for success and recognition.
- Use of humor and cordial, warm interaction with the students should be consistently injected into the classroom dialogue where appropriate.
- If the safety of students appears threatened, even remotely, obtain help immediately.
- Provide continuity in your daily lesson presentations.
- Keep accurate student records.
- Keep parents informed of any discipline, academic, or related problems.
- Promote class interaction and cooperative endeavors.
- Do not insult or humiliate students.
- Periodically remind students of the rules, regulations, and consequences.
- Continually review your classroom management checklist and assess your strengths and shortcomings.
- Invite a colleague to visit your classroom and obtain input from him or her on what he or she observes.
- Finally, the teacher is responsible for how the classroom is managed and for promoting the dignity and learning of each student. That is your cardinal rule!

KEY QUESTIONS FOR TEACHERS

1. Could a course of study in college prepare a teacher to face violence in the classroom?

2. What effective tools does a teacher have to discipline children in the classroom?

3. How much influence do you feel a child's home environment has on classroom behavior?

4. What impact does a teacher's organizational abilities and effective classroom management skills have on students' behavior?

5. The overall climate of the classroom has a considerable influence on classroom behavior. What should the teacher do when one or two children misbehave?

6. Children must feel safe in the school building. What can teachers do to best guarantee the safety of their students?

7. Is it possible to control behavior without the use of corporal punishment?

8. Is it better for the teacher to be authoritarian in the classroom?

9. Does the principal set the climate in the school? If not, who does?

10. What do you think are the major reasons for violence in the schools?

11. Should a school be expected to have an acceptable behavior code? What items should be included in such a code?

CURRICULUM AND TEXTBOOK SELECTION: WHAT NEEDS TO BE CHANGED?

A great deal of the controversy surrounding curriculum and textbook selection has occurred in recent decades because of the hot-button issues that have affected private, religious, and public schools. These issues, which are societal concerns, include:

Abortion	Church/state relationship
Sex education	Drug use
Religious beliefs and values	American foreign and economic policies
Evolution	Race relations
Nuclear war	Teenage sex
Same-sex marriages	School violence and safety
Multicultural education	Smoking
Bilingual education	Alcohol abuse
Illegal immigration	Stem-cell research
Gay unions and relationships	Political correctness
World affairs	Legal decisions

These crucial and contemporary issues are in the forefront of our daily news coverage, and some are common items of discussion by many of our high school and middle school students, and even among some upper-grade elementary school children. In many instances, our schools today are at the center of polarized community sentiments on these topics. The hardening of sociopolitical ideological thinking by groups on the left and right is now reflected in the battle for what is appropriate content to be included in our school curriculum and textbooks.

Curriculum design and textbook selection are now seen as vehicles to promote special-interest viewpoints. Therefore, it is no surprise that our teachers and our schools are caught up in this conflict. In some instances, teachers have been activists in promoting and supporting controversial issues, both inside and outside the schoolhouse. Former Secretary of Education Rod Paige was correct when he said, "The magic of education is in the classroom." However, the magic may be flawed because:

- Textbook selection and curriculum content have been influenced by special-interest groups.
- Textbook content does not always represent truthful information; textbooks can be misleading and omit important information.
- There is an inclination for our school materials to bend to current thinking on political correctness.
- Teachers are not actively involved in the curriculum and textbook selection decision-making process.
- A handful of large publishing companies dominates the marketplace.
- Motivation to make money often takes priority over the quality of the product.
- Decisions on textbook adoption are usually made further up the administrative ladder and are not always based on sound educational considerations.

There is no doubt that the textbook publishers have one primary goal—to make a profit. Publishers simply want to know what the textbooks have to say in order to get them on state-approved lists as being eligible for purchase by school districts for use in classes. Content should be neutral or not offensive to large blocks of people or to residents living in different sections of the country. On the other hand, some texts tailor their content to reflect the general views of the largest segment of the population. Texts in social studies and biology are now particularly prone to political pressures in various parts of the country.

The issues that the authors cited at the beginning of this chapter are at the center of the conflicting opinions and positions relative to curriculum and textbook selection. This requires that our teachers use good judgment in assessing the merits of the different viewpoints. This is indeed a difficult task because teachers, like the general public, have differing opinions on these controversial issues. Who is to decide what content is in the best interests of the student?

The authors must be frank and state that these issues are so complex and the American public opinion so divided that the issues may not be resolved in the near future. American society is pluralistic, and all viewpoints should be respected. These different perspectives permeate throughout our social structure and institutions. There are really no broad-based solutions and answers to what is to be included in our curriculum and textbooks.

The courts, lobbyists (representing different special interests), state legislatures, boards of education, state departments of education, power groups, and the voters are vying with one another to make an impact on the decision-making process. What is taught in our schools and what textbooks the students will use are vital issues not only in our country but in countries throughout the world. Other countries are also faced with heated religious, political, and educational debates and conflict over the subject content to be included in textbooks and curriculum materials. This is a universally deep-rooted point of contention, anger, and hostility that has surfaced in both Western nations and in countries like China, Japan, India, Pakistan, and Middle Eastern nations.

Ideally, textbook selection should be the responsibility of the teachers. This viewpoint might be accepted if the contents meet the approval of the majority of the community, are not controversial, are educationally sound, and are upheld by the courts. However, when dealing with controversial subjects, all bets are off. For example, introducing the "new math" is not the same as including sex education in the curriculum. The latter brings angry voters to the polls.

A great deal needs to be changed about how textbooks are selected. However, in the final analysis, who presides over our courts and those who wield political, social, educational, and economic power will determine what changes occur. A great deal of subject matter content and new topics has been included in curriculum and textbooks in the past several decades—yet there is very little consensus on this subject.

The following is a checklist of questions that every teacher should consider in evaluating curriculum and textbook issues:

- What process is in place in your district regarding the approval and selection of textbooks?
- Do you feel excluded from the textbook selection process?
- What role do you play in curriculum construction and design?
- Do you believe you are qualified to participate in textbook selection and curriculum development?
- Are curriculum materials developed at the district level or at the local school?
- What criteria, if any, are used to select the textbooks?
- Who makes the final decision in textbook selection?
- Are there open faculty meetings where issues of this kind are discussed?
- How often does the school district review and evaluate textbooks used in the school?
- How often is the curriculum open to review and input from the grade/subject teacher?
- Is there an appeal process for teachers who are dissatisfied with the curriculum structure or textbooks to be used?
- Do you believe the curriculum material and textbooks selected give both sides of controversial issues? If not, should they do so?
- Are the materials age-appropriate?
- Do you feel comfortable using the materials?
- Do the materials reflect a sociopolitical or religious agenda? How do you feel, if it does?
- Is the material objective in the treatment of the subject?
- If you were the decision maker, would you select the same materials?
- What changes in the process would you suggest if asked by your board of education or superintendent?

Many states are attempting to tackle textbook selection and curriculum development issues. New guidelines are being proposed for textbook selection and specific criteria for curriculum development. These proposed changes theoretically will have an impact on developing objective, sound educational standards. Teaching controversial issues often finds little common ground, and the bottom line comes down to pseudo-intellectual or politically objective decisions that, in reality, may actually be subjective or compromised.

A final word: Regardless of which textbooks are used in a classroom, teachers often have opinions on controversial matters that spill over into actual instruction. Teachers must avoid doing this. Teachers cannot tell students in a public school that only those students who accept Jesus will receive eternal salvation. Teachers cannot discuss slavery and the civil rights struggle while urging their African American students to get even with "Whitey." Evolution is a fact. Regardless of their own religious beliefs, teachers cannot tell their public school students that evolution is simply an alternative theory to Adam and Eve, in describing who and what we are today. The classroom is a place for truth, fairness, and civility. It should not and cannot be turned into a bully pulpit in which students are indoctrinated into a particular point of view.

KEY QUESTIONS FOR TEACHERS

1. Is an education possible in a democratic society with restrictions on textbook selections?
2. Should there be restrictions on subjects covered in the classroom?
3. Should there be approved lists of textbooks?
4. Can the truth be taught using biased textbooks? Should the teacher point out the biases?
5. Should the teacher be aware of the community viewpoint on a particular subject and teach that viewpoint?
6. A teacher should be aware of all viewpoints on a given subject. What is your responsibility to air all sides? Are all sides of an issue equally valid?

7. Do you feel you, as a classroom teacher, have a say in textbook selection?

8. If your students are exposed to one-sided views, what should you do?

9. What should be your role as a teacher in presenting your own personal point of view on given subjects to your students?

10. What is your definition of a democratic school?

⑫

NATIONAL STANDARDS: WHAT ARE THE DANGERS?

The need for national standards for schools, teachers, and students arises from the concept that expectations for student performance can and should be achieved at the highest level possible in all the schools in the United States. The opportunity for students to have access to a more challenging, uniform, and complete curriculum and an ability to learn and achieve at a high level of performance can be initiated by instituting national standards in the United States.

Curriculum standards could specify what students should be taught at each grade level and what they should be expected to know and how that knowledge can be measured. These standards would be based on the educational goals of the system as a whole. The plan for national standards could detail the selection of the curriculum materials and the content of the curriculum. It could also detail the educational requirements for all of the teachers. Teachers would have to have knowledge of the content in order to properly teach it to their students. They would also have to be responsible for learning how to use the curriculum materials and how to make sure that the curriculum content would be taught accurately, uniformly, and completely. Theoretically, this would ensure that each student in the United States would be getting the same level of instruction and opportunity as any other student.

There are, indeed, many positive features of instituting national standards for education. However, from the authors' viewpoint, history tells us to be very cautious when educational standards are centralized or controlled by the government. Let us not forget the lessons that we have learned from history. Consider the results when dictatorial governments, such as Mussolini's Italy, Hitler's Germany, Stalin's Soviet Union, and Japan's imperial regime controlled the educational systems. Dissent and different opinions are not tolerated in today's world in countries such as North Korea, China, Pakistan, Saudi Arabia, and Iran, where the education is centralized and the government has total control of the education of its youth. In these countries, there is only one way to do things. Everyone must comply with the dictates of the central government.

Today, even in democratic countries like Japan, England, France, and Italy, centralization of educational standards can pose dangers. An example of one of these dangers is that standards imposed by the government can overlook the need to be able to individualize situations in which both students and teachers. Standardization can cause a situation where one can lose sight of the need for allowances to be made for different positions and situations. Standardizations can bypass the need to provide opportunities for both teachers and students to be unique individuals who are critical thinkers and who can challenge the status quo. A very important question is: Can a democracy thrive when national educational standards are imposed on its citizens?

Have your ever wondered what schools would be like if national standards were imposed upon all of the schools in the country? Theoretically, national standards could be imposed for every subject that is taught in the school and for the teachers of these subjects. Standards could also be imposed for all of the books used to teach children. In this example, every school would have to teach the same curriculum, using the same books. Moreover, what if the U.S. government were to suddenly set standards on such things as what materials each school must provide for students? Standards could dictate that every biology class would have to provide a microscope for each student. Consider another illustration: What if the government instituted a standard that stated that, in every mathematics class, there had to be one computer for every student or that class size could not exceed 20 students? Each standard would result in a series of questions and controversies, and certainly would cost an enormous amount of money.

One question that arises is how we look at the minimum standards of education that each teacher should possess. It is easy for the authors to say that all teachers should have a bachelor's degree from an accredited college. What about the nature of the courses that the prospective teacher takes in the college to earn the degree? A multitude of colleges in the United States offer a bachelor's degree. In fact, it is possible to earn a degree without ever attending a single class in person, if one earns the degree via distance learning programs. What about the standards of the college itself? Is the college using highly selective criteria to choose students, or is it a nonselective process that allows students to attend just because they apply? The minimum standards of each selection would have to take into account many issues that would separate teacher candidates from the other applicants.

If minimum standards were to be enforced, the first thing to be evaluated would be the quality of the degree that the teacher earned. An important issue would be the quality of the degree with which the students present themselves. How would that be evaluated? What are the standards of the college they attended? What criteria were utilized in the selection of students? What criteria were used to select the teachers or the curriculum? We would all like teachers to come from a high-quality undergraduate program. We would hope that the graduates would, at the very least, speak and write the English language well and have a good understanding of communication and a good personality.

Another question that might arise about standardization is this: Is it easier to standardize a test than it is to standardize teachers? We give a test and make the assumption that all students in a given grade have been taught the same subject matter, equally well, and under similar conditions. Then we compare the scores that the students achieve by grade, school, and state. The students, the schools, and their grades will almost always differ.

Why is there so much variation in the scores and the knowledge base that students possess? Is this because of the teachers and their teaching style? Or is it because of the students and their environments at home and at the school? We tend to blame the home, the teachers, and the students for these differences. However, it could be possible that differences may stem from the curriculum or the textbooks used. The differences can also stem from the teachers, their own quality of education, their teaching style, or their understanding of the curriculum content. Can we assume that everything was equal in content from one classroom to another or from one school to another?

Everyone—parents, politicians, the business community—is concerned with what is taught in the schools that our children attend. As we noted, the curriculum that is taught is one of the most important issues. The ideas of what should be taught in the schools vary across the board depending upon whom you are asking. Everyone has his or her own idea of what should be taught. Another issue that we can see in the United States is a feeling that national curriculum standards would involve the 50 states giving up much of their control over local schools. There are over 15,000 school boards in 50 states. These school boards seem to think that having national standards would spell their doom, their demise. The school boards fear that there would be no further need for them to exist if national standards were adopted.

Although many problems are associated with national standards, there is still a general consensus that there is a definite need for them in each of our courses of study in our schools. In fact, there was an attempt to raise the academic standards by the federal government during the presidential administrations of both Bushes, as well as during the Clinton administration. The best example of this came during the George W. Bush administration, when the Goals 2000: Educate America Act was passed. The attempt to institute common standards did not succeed, one important reason being that too many restrictions were placed on how test results were to be used. Another reason was that there was too much politics involved, and this resulted in no real implementation of the Goals 2000 blueprint.

Diane Ravitch, in an article published by the Brookings Institute in 1996, gave several suggestions that she felt would help the government try to institute these standards. Ravitch suggested that these standards:

- should be restricted in number
- should be limited to what students should know and be able to do
- should be distributed widely for comments, feedback, and revision prior to adoption

- should be field-tested
- should describe content but should not dictate pedagogy

Ravitch further adds that all children are cheated by the current low expectations in our schools.

Some people feel that a national curriculum is already in effect. The fact that we have so few large textbook publishers and national testing organizations does ensure that we have a measure of grade and subject matter expectancy and continuity. However, this is generally presumed to be at a low level of expectation. A true national standard for each subject area would raise the expectation level and ensure our schools of a more highly demanding curriculum of study for each subject.

What about standards for testing the students' knowledge? The National Assessment of Educational Progress (NAEP) produces tests that expect a higher level of achievement. Some states have adopted these tests as being the unofficial standard for specific subjects. The test scores can be used by states to see how their students compare with students in other states.

Many states have their own tests that measure what their students have achieved. The state tests must conform to the highest standards possible in that state. These state tests measure what the students have learned within the guidelines of their standardized curricula.

If national standards are created for all courses of study, national standards could be applied to all institutions that train teachers. It could be a means of improving the education for teachers in our country. It seems only natural that setting standards for courses would help set standards for teacher education courses. This, in turn, could raise the standards for becoming a teacher, and make the job of becoming one resemble more closely those standards for joining other professions. Harvard's Ron Ferguson found that teacher quality, as measured by licensing exams and level of education, was the strongest single predictor of how a student will perform in school.

Any educational reform needs to be concerned with standards. It also needs to be concerned with what it is that we want our students to learn in each subject in school. The following questions must be considered and answered. What should an educated elementary school student know? What should an educated high school student know? What should an educated college student know? How do we define "educated"?

All standards involve curriculum, teacher training, and testing. We know that educational liberals oppose standards because they think that they would be set too high for poor or minority students. The controversy centers on the belief of some people that it is best to institute a system that has lower standards so that we can accommodate the minority student or the economically deprived. Some people are of the opinion that higher standards would be the norm, and the minority student or the economically deprived student must aspire to attain the same level of competency.

Another issue to contend with is that some people on the political right fear that national standards will take away the educational powers of our states and force the raising of taxes to support a more equal distribution of wealth. This line of reasoning would look at equalizing all school situations, no matter where the school is located or what the economic makeup of the area may be. Every school would have the same financial backing, no matter what the economic makeup of the given community.

Both sides ignore the fact that the schools must raise and equalize the standards or they will continue to have huge differences in achievement. If the schools do not raise their standards across the board, there will continue to be a great disparity of information that the student is taught and learns.

Everyone wants to get into the act. Everyone has varying ideas about what constitutes the appropriate level of education that schools should provide. As we have noted earlier, education is very much the domain of politicians, parents, foundations, and the business community. The setting of standards is what becomes confusing and difficult, considering all of the different input provided from the different groups.

The authors believe that national standards would enhance the possibility of teaching being recognized as a profession. Edward Rozychi says in the spring 1997 issue of *Educational Horizons* that having national standards "makes it easier to develop teacher-training programs and devise means for helping future teachers bring their students up to these standards."

Some people might say that this is a federal government problem or some might think that standards of education fall under the heading of a local problem. The authors feel it is a problem for our country. The first step in instituting national standards can be accomplished by raising the quality and training of our teachers. Once this is accomplished, the question of national standards for our schools will be on its way to being answered. The education and training of teachers will directly affect the way in which teachers can help to educate others.

Teachers have a stake in the adoption of national standards. It is a way to raise the status of their profession in the true sense of the word. First, however, they must raise their own educational standards. Obviously, this issue will seriously divide our nation—a nation already divided on so many subjects.

It should be remembered that there is already a national standard applied to schools in the United States that makes our country unique. We are the only society in the world that determines its educational success by the percentage of entering kindergarten students who attend some form of postsecondary school 13 years later. No other country determines the success or failure of its schools by using such a standard. Is this an appropriate measure of success? Perhaps such a standard does not truly measure subject content mastery, but it does indicate the importance that our country places on attending postsecondary schools.

KEY QUESTIONS FOR TEACHERS

1. Should there be national standards instituted for all courses and grades?
2. Is it possible to compare students in different types of schools, such as public or private, through test results?
3. Can we compare the academic achievement of students in different schools who live in different states and are taught different curricula?
4. Should a national standard be designed without paying attention to its political impact?
5. Do you think it is possible to combine national standards with state requirements?

6. National standards are considered by many on both the political left and right to be wrong for our society. What are your views?

7. National standards for all subjects could raise standards for low achievers and high achievers. Explain your views on this comment.

8. If the United States were to have a national standard for teaching science, for example, would it be possible to satisfy the beliefs of different religious groups?

9. Do you think that your community would be satisfied with higher standards for teachers?

10. Could the United States become a dictatorship if it had national standards for all subjects and schools?

11. Which is more important: a freely constructed curriculum or a single, national standard? What are the implications for each of these two choices?

13

TESTS AND OTHER EVALUATION TOOLS: ARE THEY FAIR?

Throughout their careers, teachers will be faced with administering tests and making judgments about their students' performance. The current reality today is that, although testing is directed at students, it is the teacher as much as the student who is being evaluated by the level of performance that the students achieve on tests. The student evaluation process may determine whether the teacher is granted tenure, transferred to a different teaching assignment, or possibly even be terminated.

How well students perform on tests will often shape school board, administrator, teacher, and parent relationships. Test scores play a more important role now than ever before in determining student promotion and retention. Consequently, the teacher's overall student performance, the total grade-level performance of students, and the scores of students on standardized tests are often even published in the local newspapers. The anxiety teachers face, given the issuance of public reports evaluating schools and grade-level achievements of students, is beyond imagination. Hard questions are frequently being asked relative to testing strategies being employed in our schools, as well as the effectiveness of the teacher and principal.

Teachers are raising questions about their role in determining which tests are to be used. Furthermore, how often should students be tested—every academic year, every other year, or quarterly? Should the educational establishment rely solely on standardized tests or should results from teacher-made daily or weekly tests carry equal weight?

The authors must point out that both teacher-made tests and standardized tests have strengths and weaknesses. The validity and reliability of many standardized achievement tests are being questioned. Do these tests favor middle- and upper-class students? Should students be denied a high school diploma even though they have passed all their required subjects but fail the required standardized tests for graduation? Why ignore teacher-made tests? Are some students better test-takers than others? Is it fair to judge a teacher's performance by the standardized test results of students? Some of these questions are currently in litigation. Furthermore, who should prepare these tests? As already pointed out, teachers are usually excluded from this task, but private, profit-making educational corporations are in the business of developing standardized tests.

Do we really want to take advantage of the teacher's expertise in making judgments about student performances? Do some students have abilities that cannot be measured by paper-and-pencil tests? If we only use standardized tests and force the teachers to teach to these tests, we may be destroying the very fabric of our learning and teaching process.

Our preference is for a system that employs both teacher-made tests and standardized tests in the evaluation of student progress. The passage of the No Child Left Behind (NCLB) Act in 2001 is a step in the right direction, but let us utilize all the means available to us in the evaluation process. If there is a disparity between teacher-made test scores and standardized achievement results, we need to ask why. These test scores could differ significantly or validate one another. The authors are indeed conflicted by the notion that teacher-made tests should carry little or no weight in promotion and graduation policies. The human element should be very much a part of the evaluation process.

It is our opinion that national and state standards are needed, but that they should be used in conjunction with other data. The authors are also aware that a serious dispute is taking place between some states and the federal government about who should be primarily responsible for education. There are also disputes about the truthfulness of some states' reporting data relative to the federal standards and student test results. The pressure for students to achieve seems to be mounting not only on teachers but also on principals, superintendents, and state departments of education as well.

Teachers today are caught between the ideas that standardized tests should be utilized to measure student progress and that they should be used to evaluate their own classroom effectiveness and accountability. The view that teacher-made tests and local examinations are not as rigorous as the standardized examinations is held by many educators. Also, there are those who believe that some states and teachers mislead the public about their students' success. As long as a teacher's performance is tied to student success, this issue will not disappear from the educational scene. The question, however, is if these two issues can be separated. We need objective outside criteria as well as in-house measurements for student and teacher evaluations.

It is no surprise that a great deal of anxiety has surfaced in the teaching ranks about what kinds of measurement tools should be employed to evaluate student progress. It is clear, however, that student achievement in the United States does not compare favorably with test results of students attending schools in other industrialized nations. This becomes even more evident when comparing the financial resources our nation allocates to education compared to the smaller per-pupil expenditure of nations whose students seem to surpass the test scores of American students.

There are also other problems with standardized tests. Some students simply do not test well. Students can be affected by test anxiety. The result of this is that the student has an inaccurately low score that does not reflect the true nature of the student's knowledge or ability. Another issue is that the teachers can change their curriculum so that the students will score higher on standardized tests.

Another issue is that students can guess at their answers. There is very little penalty, if any, for guessing right or wrong answers. What is most unfair is the fact that considerable preparation for the test can be undertaken. Students can take additional classes where preparation for particular tests is provided. Therefore, there is no uniformity in how much "prep" time is allocated for test preparation. Prep time can indeed influence the test score.

On the other hand, the teacher-made test is based on the content that the teacher has covered on the subject in class. It is not given to a randomized sample and could be administered as an oral test or include multiple-choice, essay, or true/false questions. Any combination of the above could also be used to compose a test. The teacher-made test given in a class could tell the teacher what needs the students have concerning the subject matter. Of course, a teacher-made test may be unfair if it includes only a few questions the students could answer or it includes difficult material or material not yet presented to the students. The teacher is personally involved both in teaching the students and administering the test to determine what the students have learned. Ongoing observations by classroom teachers should not be replaced by standardized test scores.

Do we really want to take advantage of the teacher's expertise in making judgments about tests? On the other hand, if we use standardized tests and force the teachers to teach to the tests, we are destroying the very fabric of our learning and teaching process.

Another aspect of testing is the controversy that surrounds college admissions. Should the Scholastic Aptitude Test (SAT) continue to be used as one of the measurements for student selection to our universities and colleges? There are those who believe that the SAT may be an objective measure of academic achievement but that it discriminates against minority and economically disadvantaged students. There are educators who want the SAT to be closely tied to the high school curriculum. The authors contend that no human measurement is perfect, but when the SAT is utilized with other criteria, such as subject grades, recommendations, personal interviews, and extracurricular activities, whatever flaws it possesses will hopefully be counterbalanced by these other factors. It is interesting to note that some private and public colleges and universities are no longer requiring the SAT examination for admission. Approximately 25% of the top liberal arts colleges have made the SAT examination optional. The *New York Times* reported on August 31, 2006, that such colleges as Mount Holyoke, Middlebury, Hamilton, Union, Bates, Providence, George Mason, Hobart, and Smith no longer require the SAT for admission.

The problem is compounded when the SAT score carries the greatest weight for college admission and student grades are often ignored. This is when a clash between the various factions supporting or opposing the SAT educational measurement tool comes to a head. There are institutions that claim that high SAT scores do not guarantee admission, but they certainly play an important role in the selection process.

Teachers and the SAT test, in some respects, have become mortal enemies. Schools of education have been criticized for the low SAT scores of many of their applicants compared with candidates to other professional schools. This is also true when the comparison is made for admission to graduate schools where the Graduate Record Examination (GRE) is administered. Teachers again score lower than other graduate school applicants. The lower test scores at both the graduate and undergraduate levels raise questions about the quality of applicants to the teaching profession.

As has already been reported, teachers are under pressure to be held accountable for their students' performance on standardized tests for K–12. The criticism is also applicable to the students' performance on the SAT test. Teachers will have to face this reality and will have to come to grips with the issues related to accountability. However, responsibility must be shared with school administrators, parents, policymakers, and legislators.

It seems quite unfair that standardized tests measure only one kind of ability. Robert Sternberg of Yale University points this out in his *Successful Intelligence: How Practical and Creative Intelligence Can Determine Success in Life*. The central question discussed in this book is: How can you determine whether or not a particular person will have future success in life?

Sternberg believes that more than the traditional "analytical" questions should be asked on tests. He believes that three types of intelligence should be measured: analytic, creative, and practical. Sternberg has stated that current IQ tests measure only analytical intelligence. Analytical tests would not measure a person's ability to be creative, to be self-motivated, or to be able to persevere in professional pursuits. Adding in those factors would help identify students who are talented in these other ways.

Just as present IQ tests measure only one type of intelligence—analytical, in general—standardized tests measure only mastery of traditional subject matter. Practical intelligence—or measuring analytical skills—does not correlate with how well a person will do in life, nor will it better predict job success. As noted earlier, all standardized tests measure similar skills and are highly intercorrelated.

We "lose" a lot of talented people because often we fail to identify students who are creative and practical. A person can do well in the practical area or creative area and not do well in the analytic area. Any testing program that only measures one kind of ability has left out a significant portion of the population.

The authors obviously see evidence of problems that can arise if we are to rely on test scores that measure one's ability and then project the success of the student using only these test scores for predicting that student's future success. We may create a situation in which people with skills in one area only will be obtaining better career opportunities.

IQ measured by only one kind of intelligence will not tell us enough about the total potential of the individual student. We continuely hear about students who had low or mediocre SAT scores and yet do quite well in college and graduate school. They are usually very motivated and creative people. They can go on to have successful, rewarding careers. Then there are always the students who get very high SAT scores and yet seem to fail at everything they do.

The bottom line is that the scores resulting from traditional testing and IQ scores should not be the determining factors in the selection process when we are trying to determine the future success of a particular student. We should take into account other factors, such as special talents, creativity, grades, motivation, work experience, successful relationships, self-esteem, self-discipline, and goals that the student has set for himself or herself when we try to project future success.

It should be further pointed out that there are 50 million immigrants out of a total of 300 million people in the United States. Many of these immigrants and their children either do not speak English at all or have limited proficiency in English. Consequently, it is no surprise that our schools have found that the test scores of such children are low and that they have a high dropout rate. Also, a high percentage of our immigrant population are unskilled workers, and they usually fall into the lower economic niche.

Research has shown that success in schools is highly correlated to social and economic class and English-speaking skills. The standardized tests administered in our schools reflect economic bias. They also have cultural and racial limitations. Because the United States now has the largest percentage of immigrants in our history, schools have additional responsibilities in assimilating our young immigrant population. How we evaluate the potential of this large group of individuals, who are in a strange land with a different language and with different values, mores, and expectations, is a complex challenge. Standardized testing may not be the answer when we consider the evaluation of our immigrant groups.

KEY QUESTIONS FOR TEACHERS

1. A teacher believes that IQ scores are highly related to school achievement and therefore grades his or her pupils according to this score. What is your opinion about this?
2. Should a school curriculum be based on the content of standardized tests?
3. Should classroom rank be given more weight than rank based on standardized test scores? Why?
4. If a student does well in school, based on teacher tests, should a state-administered test determine whether he or she should graduate?
5. How important should school grades be in terms of determining admission to college?
6. If teacher grades are important in the college admission process, does this lead to grade inflation?
7. If a high school grade point average is a better predictor of college success, why should SAT scores be used?
8. How much are income and minority group membership related to school achievement?

9. Should teachers, in general, have higher SAT scores and higher college grades than their students? Is it possible for a genius to be taught by an average teacher?

10. A good test tells the teacher what it is the student knows and does not know. Are tests used for that purpose? If not, for what purposes are they used?

14

THE GRADING SYSTEM:
HOW DO YOU HANDLE IT?

The grading system used in the schools in this country, from kindergarten to the graduate level, is in turmoil. Perhaps the greatest pressure placed on a teacher is assigning a grade. Over the years, this issue has been further complicated by the heightened expectations of students and parents, the involvement of the courts, and the lack of a clear definition of what a specific grade really represents.

When grades are compared to learning outcomes, the authors have concluded that parents may be more concerned about grades. Excellent grades are the tickets to higher education, scholarships, admission to superior-ranking colleges, and initial job placement. Students from the first grade on are bombarded by parents to get good grades in school. When a child comes home with a report card, the parent asks, "What are your grades?" Infrequently is the question asked, "What have you learned in school?" Grades are very much more valued than learning. The grading system that has been used in America may vary from decade to decade, but the pressure to attain good grades permeates all the systems that have been used.

The authors have observed how many teachers and college professors assign grades. It has been clear to us that, regardless of the grading system utilized, in the last analysis, it is the individual instructor's educational philosophy, the school's grading policy, and personal beliefs and values that will ultimately determine the grade given a student. Grading is a very personal perspective on the academic achievement of each student.

A great deal has been written about the importance of fair grading. School districts and even some colleges have elaborate guidelines for grading. Many schools and colleges also have statements concerning students' rights. Generally, teachers' grades are seldom overturned unless the grade can be viewed as capricious, arbitrary, biased, or unable to be substantiated by objective criteria. Yet there are subjective considerations that are difficult to measure, such as the quality of oral reports, classroom dialogue, and even essay test responses. At the lower grades, pupil attitudes, getting along with peers, ability to work independently, neatness, punctuality, and completing assignments on time are just a few of the items on which teachers must base their judgment, but all have elements of subjectivity.

The authors support clear grading guidelines, not only for each school but for particular subjects. Yet attempting to establish standard norms is not an easy task, for there are so many expectations. Nevertheless, we believe policy statements and guidelines serve as good benchmarks for both teachers and students. Students will feel more confident when they know the factors that will constitute their grades. Teachers, too, will at least know the general school policies and thus avoid needless student grievances and appeals.

Obviously, grade policies cannot cover every detail and situation. The teacher needs some flexibility in determining a student's grade. Frequently it has been noted that teachers may have children with similar test scores and yet, because of the many other variables in the learning process, a teacher will assign different grades for what may appear to be comparable achievement.

Coupled with the complex issues associated with assigning grades, there is also considerable concern about grade inflation. The authors believe that grades at all levels of American education are inflated. A colleague of the authors who is teaching at a major university pointed out that no longer is there a "gentleman's C" in the grading system. The students all now expect to receive at least a B grade and, in some instances, nothing but an A will suffice. Grade inflation appears to exist not only at our colleges and universities but at all grade levels. We have never been told by a student that the A grade received was not deserved. Yet, we have had students with B+ grades who were vehement in voicing their disappointment because they did not receive an A. In the final analysis, we think, a B+ is a pretty good grade.

For decades the authors have questioned the way teachers grade their students. This issue pertains equally to public, private, and religious educational institutions. In our experiences, we have witnessed the lowering of standards and educational expectations, while at the same time a grade explosion has taken place in our schools

The grading system is indeed in need of a review. The system now includes such symbols as A, B, C, D, F, or E, V, S, I, and U. In addition to letter grades, some schools and higher education institutions have used numerical grades. The grading system in our schools and colleges has been in flux for years. With all the confusion about grades, the authors believe that the classroom teacher's assessment gives a relatively good profile as to how children are doing in school. The everyday contact between teacher and pupil reinforces the likelihood that the teacher's judgments are a reliable picture of the total classroom performance of the child. As the authors have already pointed out, teachers do have shortcomings and professional limitations. Parents and students need to understand that grading is a tough assignment, as it is in every profession and job. The hardest challenge a professional football coach faces is his or her evaluation of the players' performances.

Perhaps the most important consideration in grading should be: What is the purpose of grading? Grading is an instrument that very succinctly attempts to communicate the academic achievements of the students by a simple letter or numerical designation. Although the grading system is faced with many problems, the system is essentially used universally in our schools and colleges and universities.

As teachers, the authors did use their individual judgment, but utilized all the data that were available to them to arrive at a realistic and hopefully fair grade. We did not find grading to be one of the particularly attractive features of our duties as teachers. In fact, the competitive dimension of the grading system serves both as a catalyst as well as a hindrance in the learning and teaching process. We found the so-called intrinsic motivation of grades to be applicable to some students and counterproductive for others. Therefore, how a teacher handles grades is a sensitive subject and should be carefully considered. Grades can be both a motivating force and yet contribute to student frustration and loss of interest in the subject. Obviously, students must earn their grades and be held accountable for their classroom performance. On the other hand, the teacher must be fair and honest with the student.

There are those critics of the American grading system who are very skeptical of teachers who use the bell curve method in their grading philosophy. This relative grading system provides no way to accurately compare students with those who are evaluated based on a standard, uniform grading system. Because of the many variables involved in grading, including the teacher's individual judgment and whether the teacher compares the students to formulate the grade, the whole system is under suspicion and scrutiny.

It is interesting to note that many college admission officers give greater weight to high grades attained from prestige high schools and do not value as highly similar grades achieved by students who attended schools without a reputation for academic excellence. A student who receives an A grade point average from Stuyvesant High School, a school for academically gifted students in New York City, undoubtedly will be given special preference when compared to a student from a small rural high school in Appalachia or a student from an inner-city high school.

Grades, for all intents and purposes, do not give a clear individual achievement profile and often can be misleading. The school from which the student receives his or her grades can at times be more important than the grades achieved. The school's reputation does play a role in many colleges' and universities' admission considerations.

Grades are very important because, along with standardized tests, they play an important role in college selection, employment opportunities, and career choices. Thus, teachers are faced with a tremendous task in assessing student achievement and in assigning grades. There never has been a perfect instrument that could be utilized to make objective grade evaluation decisions. Subjectivity and bias in assigning grades will be with us during our lifetime. However, strategies still need to be developed to further strengthen the grade evaluation process. It is our belief that the teaching profession must accept, in principle, the concept of accountability and must work to develop a universally equitable grade model. Time will tell how successful we are.

The authors do not want to close this chapter without pointing out the following: Grading is a complex process, and we call can agree that it is not foolproof. But when a student consistently receives comparable grades from various teachers, whether they are A or C grades, the grading process appears to be validated for that school setting. However, when one goes beyond a particular school, comparative grades are more complex to assess.

When one tries to explain the grade inflation issue, societal philosophies leave a strong imprint on educational policies. There is an apparent view that every student must be successful and given the benefit of the doubt. Cultural, economic, and political considerations also play a decisive role as to why some students complete high school and receive a high school diploma but are still unable to read at a sixth-grade level or can even be functionally illiterate. Simply stated, there is often considerable hesitation by teachers and administrators to give low grades and face angry parents and students. The elaborate grievance procedures instituted in some high schools, universities, and colleges contribute to the teachers' reluctance to get involved with contested grades.

Grade inflation is a disturbing development but, in the last analysis, the teacher is still in the best position to fairly evaluate the student. However, our educational establishment needs to assess those forces and pressure groups that may be contributing to grade inflation. There is also the need to carefully study teacher attitudes and instructional practices at all grade levels, including higher education. Our educational system needs a functional grading system that reflects true student achievement.

One final note: Teachers who hold the line on grade inflation are under severe pressure from parents and often receive little support from the school administration. This should not be the case. Teachers should not be under pressure to give grades of A or B to all of their students.

KEY QUESTIONS FOR TEACHERS

1. Do you think it is more appropriate for grading to be based on a local norm or a national norm?

2. What do you think of a ranking system of grading where the brightest student in the class is given the rank of 1 and the lowest achieving student the rank of 25 (if there are 25 students in the class)?

3. All students must know the standards for which they are graded. If this is the case, the students will know their grades are fair. Is this an appropriate expectation of your classroom grading system?

4. Questions regarding the grading system could influence the curriculum. How much influence should grading have on the curriculum?

5. Essay questions are thought to be more appropriate for students with high academic ability. If this is true, what effect will this have on your grading?

6. Are you considered a "hard marker" by your students?

7. If you give a grade of A to most students, how will such a policy affect your teaching practices?

8. The "normal curve" concept holds that only 50% of the population is above average. How could you measure whether you have an above-average or below-average class? Should your grading system conform with the theory?

9. If your students learn all that you have taught them and earn an A on your test, is it possible that you have not sufficiently challenged your students?

10. Should the standard for grading your students be: "Have the students learned to the best of their abilities?"

15

TEACHING CONTROVERSIAL ISSUES: SHOULD THEY BE INCLUDED IN THE CURRICULUM?

When it comes to controversial issues, teachers are placed in very difficult positions. Our nation today is divided by conflicting, deep-rooted positions and opinions, and teaching the merits of different points of view requires extreme caution and good judgment. Because there is this fierce battle of philosophical, historical, religious, social, cultural, economic, political, and scientific issues in our society, a teacher will need to carefully navigate classroom dialogue through very stormy weather. Consensus building is often an impossible task for the teacher to achieve.

However, what is very important is that the teacher has helped each student to gain a sound perspective of the issues, obtain the prerequisite knowledge base to better understand the conflicting viewpoints, and then come to a rational conclusion. The teacher is the catalyst who, through key pivotal questions, helps each student to engage the tough positions being addressed in the classroom.

When a teacher approaches a unit of study that includes topics considered controversial, such as sex education, drugs, politics, historical events, ethics, reproduction, economic policies, multiculturalism, and immigration, students must be prepared to handle such discussions, and the ground rules must be fair and balanced. There is no point in addressing these issues unless the goals of promoting mutual understanding, respect, and tolerance are underscored in classroom discussion, although the topics may be controversial.

The authors have serious reservations about introducing controversial topics in the early grades. Teachers need to ask the following questions:

- At what grade level should a specific topic be introduced?
- What content should be included?
- What should be the frequency and duration for these topics to appear in the curriculum?
- How should these topics be taught?
- Why should they be taught?
- What reading materials should be recommended?

It is the authors' opinion that elementary grades are not an appropriate forum to introduce controversial subjects without parental input and special review. There is a heavy burden placed on whether educators are using common sense, good judgment, sensitivity, and age-appropriate subjects prior to making decisions about implementing subject content in any curriculum. Regardless of the grade, teachers must carefully consider that comprehensive steps must be undertaken so that stakeholders in the school have had input prior to reaching formal decisions. If our society is going to avoid harsh, critical clashes over issues presented in our schools, at the very least, open discussion and information sessions need to be made available to parents. Teachers should receive special training in the teaching of controversial issues. We must remember that grades K–6 are the formative years in which children develop opinions that sometime last a lifetime.

Teachers must develop well-thought-out lesson plans with clearly stated objectives and a road map of sequential steps to be undertaken in driving the lesson. Critical pivotal questions need to be thought out prior to the lesson, and an ample opportunity for student discussion and activities must be provided. Teachers must give careful thought to any positions that they plan to articulate in the classroom related to the subject being discussed. Teachers must always focus on the issues and not on whether a student agrees or disagrees with them. Teachers should not dominate the discussion but give the students every chance to participate. A classic error that should always be avoided by teachers is to disrespect a student's opinion or ridicule someone who fails to comprehend the issue. Teachers need to establish a warm, friendly climate in the classroom.

The issues surrounding the teaching of controversial topics, which issues should be discussed, and at what grade level to start, appear to be a never-ending battle that may not be resolved in the near future—or ever, for that matter.

Related to the teaching of controversial issues in the classroom, and something that already has resulted in considerable litigation by various constituencies, some teachers introduce controversial subjects outside their subject area license and then give their personal opinions to the students in their classroom. The authors believe this is not an acceptable practice. Those teachers violate the public trust when they use their privileged position to hold their students hostage to listen to their particular viewpoints. This is where teachers create harsh confrontation and conflict and are attacked for overstepping their professional obligations. Public school teachers must not impose their own personal views on their students. For example, creationism may be a valid personal belief, but a teacher is bound by facts and data. Thus, evolution must be taught as a fact and not as an alternative theory.

One of the most difficult questions facing Americans today is what defines a controversial issue. In one community, region, or state, some issues are considered rational subjects that are often included into curricula without heated discussion by boards of education. In other localities, similar issues are hotly contended, and fierce political debates divide communities. The social and political divide in our nation is becoming a serious matter, causing continuous confrontation between our citizens. No amount of compromise or persuasion is going to bring people together from both sides of the sociopolitical spectrum. Is the schoolhouse the place for controversial issues to be discussed? This has been the case in many parts of our country as well as in different times. Does anyone need to be reminded about the prominence of the Scopes trial in Tennessee in 1925? In case you forgot, Scopes lost his job for teaching the concept of evolution.

Our society does indeed need critical thinkers, and our teachers need to play an important role in developing the basic skills required for a student to be a critical thinker in all fields of endeavor. The authors endorse the teaching of controversial issues in the classroom with the specific conditions that they have outlined in this chapter.

The authors conclude this chapter by stating that students get really enthusiastic and welcome controversial issues being discussed in the classroom. However, these issues should be raised within the subject being taught and be age appropriate.

KEY QUESTIONS FOR TEACHERS

1. Should controversial topics be discussed in a classroom regardless of subject content?
2. If the community agrees that certain subjects should not be discussed by teachers, and a student brings up one of the issues in school, what should the teacher do?
3. Would you have a list of topics or issues that you would forbid to be discussed in class?
4. If the answer to the above question is "yes," what topics would be included on such a list?
5. What is your opinion about the theory of evolution? What if the community believes in creationism?
6. Should a teacher be neutral on an issue about which the community feels strongly?
7. What kind of preparation should the college provide the prospective teacher in the teaching of controversial subject matter?
8. Is it possible for students to listen to the pros and cons of an emotional and controversial issue?
9. Is there a way to teach critical thinking without studying a particularly controversial issue? How?
10. Is teaching a controversial subject worth risking your job because of difficulties you may encounter from the community in which you teach?

16

HETEROGENEOUS AND HOMOGENEOUS GROUPINGS: WHICH DO YOU PREFER?

For almost 100 years, the grouping of students has been one of the most controversial issues facing schools. There is no consensus on this issue, and the debate continues to this day. The pros and cons of the best educational practice for grouping students have also taken on a sociopolitical dimension, an occurrence that further complicates student placement.

The essential issue of grouping must focus on the kinds of learning and teaching environments that are best for our students. Because our diversified student population has many special needs, interests, and abilities, one broad stroke will not suffice in attempting to answer this question. Nevertheless, educators and educational critics often present an "either-or" solution to the problem.

Classifying students is a difficult task. Educators have attempted to categorize students in an assortment of groups. These classifications cover the educational gamut and include the gifted, slow learners, students with special needs and learning disabilities, average achievers, students with special artistic talents, students who need instruction in English as a second language, and so forth. For years, the sexes were often separated into special gender schools and classrooms. In New York City, like many other school districts, there are special schools for gifted students in science and engineering, such as Stuyvesant and the Bronx

High School of Science. Numerous magnet and charter schools now exist, many with specializations that focus on careers and the special interests and needs of students. There are even special schools for students with emotional and behavioral problems. Within this large pool of students, educators have attempted to group students in either heterogeneous or homogeneous schools and classroom settings, depending on the students' individual needs. It certainly has not been an easy assignment for the teaching profession.

Supporters of heterogeneous groupings say the best-performing students in the class will serve as role models for other students who may not have the same degree of motivation or abilities. According to the supporters of heterogeneous groupings, the talented academic students will push their less talented classmates to work harder in their academic studies. Furthermore, students with diversified backgrounds and abilities represent the spirit of American democracy and the melting pot, and they should not be isolated from their fellow students. On occasion, we believe that homogeneous grouping is justified because of the specialized attention required for students who are severely sight-impaired, hearing-impaired, as well as those in need of remedial assistance.

On the other hand, proponents of homogeneous groupings believe that the bright students in the class may be slowed down by their less gifted classmates. Teachers may be required to spend an inordinate amount of time with the less talented students and provide less time enriching the academic experience for the higher-achieving students. It is obvious that teaching a class with 25 students of varying abilities calls for a teacher with special talents and skills. Teaching today is a complex process, and the teacher is faced with a variety of student needs and many outside pressures.

During the past several decades, there has been some negative reaction to special schools, classes, and programs for the gifted. The pressure on educators was strong enough for them to begin to view gifted programs as elitist and not cost effective. Many K–12 gifted programs came under severe attack from critics. The good news is that the pendulum has now moved in the direction of recognizing that special programs are in the best interests of our talented and special needs students, so that our nation can develop *all* students to their fullest potential. More and more high schools are developing specialized courses for the gifted and are participating in advanced college placement courses. Many K–8 schools are now offering additional classes for gifted students. Homogeneous grouping is an accepted practice in many school districts.

We are witnessing the increase in homogeneous classes to help develop students' reading skills and in other subject areas. The passage of the No Child Left Behind Act has also placed greater emphasis on test results. In our opinion, homogeneous grouping, whether one likes it or not, will promote overall improved test results and improved student achievement.

The authors do not, however, recommend that all classes be homogeneous. Serious psychological damage can be inflicted if the student's self-image, identity, and confidence are eroded as a result of being in remedial and other special needs classes for too many years or even in too many such classes during the school day. It is our recommendation that the special grouping of children should be limited to no more than two or three classes in departmental subjects or two specialized groupings within the K–6 self-contained classroom. The greatest danger of homogeneous grouping, as previously pointed out, is that we cannot as teachers judge and classify our students prematurely. Particularly at the K–6 level, students often become stereotyped by teachers, lose self-respect, and have serious doubts about their ability and potential. Students have a keen sense of what grouping means and can readily comprehend the implications of it for themselves.

As far as students are concerned, most of them know who are the brightest and the slowest amongst them. In a way, this mitigates against which system of grouping is "best" for students. Whatever way students are grouped, they know who's who.

KEY QUESTIONS FOR TEACHERS

1. Do you think it is possible to teach a math course to a heterogeneous group?
2. Similarly, is it possible to teach a history course to a heterogeneous group?
3. In what ways do you think subject matter is the key to teaching a heterogeneous vs. homogeneous group?

4. Should schools, in general, group students according to ability?
5. Should grouping begin at the earliest grades?
6. Grouping usually stigmatizes students; is this a community issue, a school issue, a personal issue?
7. If schools are to teach all they can to all students, and students are to learn all they can, how can educators best communicate this concept?
8. Students and their parents recognize that they can't all be star athletes. Why then is it so difficult for many students and their parents to accept the reality that they cannot be academic stars?
9. Would you expect a teacher of violin to teach all students in the school?
10. Some countries group students after they reach grade 6 as college material, others as noncollege material. Should the American education system follow a similar plan?

17

HOMEWORK:
TOO LITTLE OR TOO MUCH?

Homework assignments are indeed a key component of the learning and teaching process. Teachers are constantly confronted with such questions as:

- What is the purpose of homework assignments?
- How much homework should be required?
- Will my child's homework be graded?
- Will the homework be counted toward the student's grade?
- Should homework assignments represent a variety of subject content learned, or based solely on the day's lesson?
- How prompt should the teacher be in reviewing the student's homework assignment and returning the corrected copy?
- Should homework be assigned over the weekends or holidays?
- How long should a student spend on one subject assignment?
- Do various subject-area teachers coordinate among themselves homework assignments in order not to overwhelm students with major projects due at the same time?
- Should homework assignments be standardized for each subject level, or should each teacher be responsible for preparing individualized assignments for each class?

- Are homework assignments discussed the following day in class?
- Should homework assignments be multiple choice, true or false, or essays?
- Should homework be tailored to each student's abilities?
- Do homework assignments allow for individual student and group work?
- Do you as the teacher have a homework assignment schedule plan for each unit and lesson plan?
- Do you explain to your students how to manage their time when they go home to do their homework assignments?
- Are you explicit when giving homework assignments?
- Do you reinforce oral assignments with specific written instructions at a language level suitable for the student?
- Are you cognizant of the time required to complete your homework assignment?
- Do you communicate with parents concerning homework issues and why homework is an important part of the learning process?

Homework in the United States should be an essential requirement of the school curriculum. For students in the United States, the school year is shorter than many other countries, ranging from 16 to 60 fewer days per academic year. Furthermore, it is also reported that American students spend only from 50 to 60% of their school day on core academic subjects when compared to students in other industrialized nations. With our limited school day and year, students need learning activities that will reinforce classroom content, motivate discovery, and broaden their knowledge base. Through meaningful homework, teachers can maximize the breadth and scope of students' core academic subjects and extend the time they devote to academic development and learning.

Parents who work all day often find that it is a burdensome task to devote time to helping their children when they come home from work. Thus, parents point out that the homework is often not checked because of the many household chores to which they must attend. This is especially true for parents who have children in elementary school. Nevertheless, homework should not be left for the late evening hours or morning hours before students go to school. There is too much tension in the morning, it is counterproductive to the students, and it adds additional pressure to their day.

Teachers need to integrate homework into their lesson plans and estimate the required time for completion. Teachers also need to coordinate these assignments with their colleagues who may also be teaching their students. Homework should always be reviewed by the teacher and returned promptly. Homework that is graded may create some tension for the students but, in our experience, it provides greater student motivation. The students and parents are more likely to take the assignment more seriously if homework is graded and returned with comments. Assignments need to be challenging and cover different types of exercises, including writing essays, book reports, answering short-answer and true-and-false questions, solving problems, performing experiments, preparing charts and graphs, writing speeches, and a host of other different learning experiences.

It is imperative that the teachers do not use homework as a vehicle to punish students or for the sole purpose of keeping them busy. Additionally, teachers should not excuse students from homework as a reward for good behavior or superior class performance. Homework should be used as an enrichment learning experience, regardless of student behavior or academic achievement. For students with different abilities, homework needs to be tailored to the individual student's achievement level and subject skill needs.

The authors reiterate that homework should be used: (1) to introduce students to new assignments or topics; (2) to provide further enrichment experience for the gifted, average, and those with special needs; (3) to reinforce both new and previous class learning and concepts; (4) to provide enrichment experience to help students to remedy academic deficiencies; and (5) to provide continuous learning beyond the normal school day.

Teachers need to work with parents so that the home is homework-friendly and time-management schedules are developed as guidelines for students. Parents must take active roles in helping their children feel comfortable in a pleasant environment where they can pursue homework assignments. Some students from economically deprived circumstances may live in crowded apartments that are not as conducive to doing homework as in a quiet, well-lit physical environment.

Teachers and parents must remember that there is a positive correlation between doing homework consistently and success in the subject. Too little or too much homework will be detrimental to the student. Although students may verbalize that they do not like homework, students generally welcome homework assignments and find them challenging. A good teacher provides homework that challenges the students and serves as an intrinsic motivator to learning.

Teachers need to spend time explaining simple rules to the students that need to be followed in order for the homework assignment to provide maximum educational value. These explanations to students should include:

- Do your homework as soon as you arrive home from school.
- Find a quiet place in your home where you will not be disturbed.
- Make sure you have proper lighting and ventilation when doing your assignment.
- Do not watch television, listen to the radio, or attempt to do other chores while doing your homework.
- Review your assignment carefully before answering the questions.
- Upon completion of the assignment, take a few moments to review your work.
- Take pride in your homework.
- Be neat in preparing your homework.
- Have a file folder specially designated for homework.
- Carefully review corrected homework from the previous day.
- Good organization and time management are essential in scheduling homework assignment work.
- Avoid interruptions from family and friends.
- Schedule free time for recreation in your schedule.

Over the years, and especially during the post–World War II period, homework has become a controversial issue in our schools. However, if our children are going to be competitive in the future global economy, we should follow the examples of such countries as Japan, South Korea, Taiwan, and India, where homework is a vital component of the learning process.

KEY QUESTIONS FOR TEACHERS

1. Should homework be a requirement for all academic subjects?
2. Homework expectations could be the basis of a classroom activity. If this is so, how should a teacher use this time to the best advantage?
3. In what ways could teachers coordinate their homework assignments with other teachers so that students are not overburdened?
4. Should homework be assigned in such a way as to ensure it can be done without considerable help from others?
5. How can the teacher be sure that the homework assignments are actually done by the student?
6. How can a teacher be sure that homework is viewed by students as an integral part of the school lesson?
7. What should be the major purpose for assigning homework?
8. Some students do not have a place or the time to do homework. Should homework be part of their school day?
9. Do you feel homework should be graded? If so, how do you distinguish work done by the student from work done with help from others?
10. Is it possible that homework interferes with the social growth of individuals?

PARENT-TEACHER-PRINCIPAL RELATIONSHIPS: CAN THEY BE EFFECTIVE?

For a school to move forward, there must be established collaboration, trust, collegiality, teamwork, common goals, and a unified mission among parents, teachers, and the principal. Effective teacher involvement is a key component in facilitating positive school-community relations.

Those who lead our schools must have their pulse on the teachers' views, perspectives, and concerns that may have an impact on their daily performance. An effective faculty must feel that they are truly partners in the educational process and that they have real opportunities to provide input in the development of school policies and decisions.

Parents must also feel that they, too, are accepted partners in formulating school decisions and strengthening the school culture. Very frequently, parents are viewed as outsiders and window dressing to demonstrate community involvement. If a school is going to have a successful outreach in the community, parents cannot be considered strangers and must be included in all aspects of the school's program. After all, it is because of their children that the school exists and school personnel have jobs. In too many instances, parents are excluded from the inner circle of the school's decision makers. School cultures that empower the school staff and parents in the organization's planning and development of the curriculum will discover a stronger commitment to the goals and objectives by these groups. Establishing good communication and developing consensus prior to making public announcements will lessen the possibility of angry teachers or parents' confronting the school administration.

With the advent of accountability, tension has developed and finger-pointing has surfaced at all segments and levels of the educational establishment. At times, it appears that there is a closing of the ranks against those who raise their voices because of job insecurity and the criticism that is directed at teachers and administrators. Accountability and performance evaluation of school personnel may hinder collegiality between parents and the school.

Both the principal and the teachers should view parental input and recommendations as positive signs of genuine interest and concern among parents. Frequently, however, such gestures can become points of contention and cause dissension and conflict. Parents' suggestions should always be welcomed and acknowledged with gratitude and appreciation. Teachers should remember that ultimately they are in control and thus should be gracious rather than abrupt with parents. Always allow parents the opportunity to share their views or concerns with you. Loss of temper or of one's emotions does not promote good rapport and may even have long-lasting, negative consequences. Respect and trust are prerequisites to all good relationships.

One of the ways to get parents actively involved is to employ them as teaching assistants. Active membership in the local Parent Teacher Association (PTA) is also another excellent avenue to build cohesiveness and collegiality between parents and teachers. Inviting parents to observe classroom instruction rather than relying only on such outdated strategies as the parent-teacher night can be very meaningful to parents. When parents do visit with a teacher, a quiet, empty office should be provided so that the parent can discuss confidential matters in private rather than doing so in the hallway or in the presence of students.

Schools must extend a warm, cordial reception to parents, especially to those parents who have difficulties speaking English. Small groups of parents should be invited to the principal's office for coffee and be given the opportunity to express their feelings, concerns, frustrations, and what they like or dislike about the school. Personal growth and development work both ways. The authors have found that they gained wisdom and a better understanding of the parents' viewpoints in these small group settings where there is personal contact.

School groups need to dialogue, discuss, and to share ideas. It is very important that rules and regulations are based on mutual self-interest and understanding. All parties, including students, need to come together as a family rather than be fragmented and unable to establish common goals. Often teachers criticize the heavy-handed style of their principal or superintendent because they feel browbeaten into implementing a program or supporting a specific policy. The chain of command may have a place, but to be an effective leader as a teacher or administrator, both techniques need to be considered. First, in the authors' opinion, the best approach is to rely on a horizontal, managerial plan where no one party is ignored and all participants can express their views without intimidation and/or fear of reprisal and where respective positions are shared and mutually accepted goals can be reached.

Many policymakers across the nation, as well as teachers, are beginning to recognize that involving all the constituent groups will bring about promising policies and practices. Societal changes require that our schools become flexible social institutions capable of including the new knowledge and learning skills necessary for future generations of students to compete in our global society. Our schools are becoming increasingly diverse, and our teachers need to be sensitive to cultural differences and promote good parent-student-teacher rapport.

Everyone likes to be included in brainstorming sessions, whether in education, business, sports, or even the military. Inclusion increases self-esteem, feeds the ego, brings new ideas to the table, and makes everyone a stakeholder in the process. By having open meetings, secret information is eliminated and greater trust among the participants, principals, teachers, and parents is established.

Let us cite an example of how a teacher should *not* relate to a parent. Many years ago, one of the authors was a pupil in the fourth grade in an elementary school in the Bronx, New York. He turned around to reply to a classmate—a simple, innocent act. The teacher had him reassigned to the third grade until one of his parents came to school to discuss his behavior with the teacher. The parent, however, had to take several hours off from work to meet with the teacher. The parent did not speak English, and it was a difficult meeting. Times have indeed changed, but basic principles of good judgment do not. We, as professional educators, always need to keep in mind the following:

- Can I handle a problem with a child without initially involving the parent?
- What really constitutes a pupil problem?
- Is the punishment reasonable for the act committed?
- What criteria should be used when sending for a parent who may have to take off from work?
- Did I thoroughly investigate the problem?
- Did I have a translator available for my conference with the parent, if the parent had limited English proficiency?
- Did I make the parent feel comfortable and convey the impression that I was there to help her or his child?
- Was the parent's respect and integrity compromised?
- Did the meeting end on friendly, positive terms?

The example given above comes under the rubric of how parents are treated in our schools. One of the important things a school can do is to ensure that pupils and parents are welcomed to the schoolhouse. Parent-teacher meetings are an important gauge to measure and evaluate how sensitive teachers are to parents, especially if they are non-English-speakers and represent different cultures, with different norms and values. The warm, caring welcome mat must be very much part of every school culture.

Parents should be invited to school not only when their children are in trouble but also when the teacher has something positive to convey. Sharing good news with a parent is an important strategy that should always be included as part of the teacher's arsenal in strengthening the teacher-parent relationship.

Obviously, giving good news to a parent is less stressful than criticism. Therefore, special consideration should be given to a first meeting. When a teacher meets someone for the first time, it will usually have a lasting impression. It is important that the teacher make every effort to connect with the parent. A teacher should not be late for the appointment; a late arrival may create tension and present an awkward first session. The initial meeting should begin on a warm, cordial exchange. A

smile goes a long way in promoting a good, healthy beginning to a relationship. Thank the parent for coming to see you. Respect and sensitivity toward the parent will go a long way in promoting good rapport. The
teacher must listen to the parent and should not interrupt when the parent is speaking. On the other hand, the teacher should not hesitate to
discuss hard issues, but must do so in a calm, caring demeanor.

KEY QUESTIONS FOR TEACHERS

1. How can your principal contribute to your working effectively
   with parents?
2. Why should parents be an integral part of a school's fabric?
3. Have you had training in interpersonal relationships?
4. How much input should a parent have on school policymaking?
5. If the PTA in your school has the power to influence your principal, is that a healthy situation?
6. Parents should be encouraged to participate in their children's
   education. Should they also participate in shaping the curriculum
   and other school policies?
7. Do private schools and religious schools encourage parent participation? In what ways?
8. In diverse communities, would the parents of the children have to
   agree as to how best the school and the parents can work together?
9. How should parent-teacher conferences be handled?
10. Would you want your school board to give more weight to parents
    than to teachers on a curriculum matter?

IV

EVOLVING ISSUES

19

THE EXTENDED SCHOOL YEAR: ARE WE READY FOR IT?

It has been estimated that about 10 million school-age children are unsupervised during after-school hours and during summer vacations. Many of these children are in need of additional tutorial help, enrichment courses, counseling, and continued exposure to the learning process. Disadvantaged students, children who come from single-family homes, newly arrived immigrants, and children with learning disabilities need every hour of instruction. The authors encourage all parents and teachers to petition their local school board to consider the extended school year.

In our many years of experience, we have witnessed teachers seeking employment during after-school hours and during the summer months. Almost half the teachers who are the breadwinners in the home seek outside employment because of inadequate salaries to support their families. These teachers seek any type of employment that they can find. It seems to us that our society needs educators who are devoting all their energies full-time to helping upgrade the educational achievement level of all our young people. It simply makes no sense that so many of our teachers must go outside their profession after school hours and during the summer months to find employment when there are so many pressing needs in the school itself.

The authors are aware that organizations such as the National Education Association (NEA) and the American Federation of Teachers (AFT) have strongly opposed any initiative to expand the school day and to extend the learning year to 11 months. Many reasons are given for objecting to this proposal. Teacher organizations are not the only ones who are raising serious objections to the extended school year. Airlines, summer camps, the travel industry, and some parent groups and especially taxpayer associations see little merit in this proposal. Research is both inconclusive and, data are limited on the value of the longer school year or extended day. Although the authors have not independently undertaken any in-depth study of these issues, common sense dictates to us that the benefits of an extended school year far outweigh the concerns that have been expressed by the opponents of this proposal. We believe teachers have been misguided and that there should be further discussion on the extended school year and the longer school day. Of course, teachers should be compensated for these extra assignments. Implementation could be phased in over a 5-year period. Parents and teachers need to be consulted and have input in the decision-making process of their respective districts.

The proponents of extending the school day and school year have cited numerous reasons why our schools should move ahead and explore implementing these programs. The arguments presented in favor of this idea include the need for our nation to be competitive in the global economy. We need to prepare intelligent, well-educated students to enter the workforce. America cannot afford to lag behind other industrial nations in educational achievement. In countries such as Japan, China, Germany, South Korea, and India, students attend classes from 216 to 243 days a year, as compared to our 180 days, and their school day is usually longer than ours. The average American student attends school from 8:30 A.M. to 3:00 P.M. In a Chinese high school, the school day begins at 8:00 A.M. and continues until 8:30 P.M. or 9:00 P.M. The schooldays do provide, however, three hours for lunch and dinner breaks.

The man/woman-power pool in America is presently composed of a high percentage of high school dropouts. It is imperative that educators address the problems associated with an unskilled labor force. Many students who graduate from high school and enter the workforce are found to be functionally illiterate by their employees. Why not give our student population, including gifted students, more enrichment experiences, as well as remedial work? If our students have a longer school day, and the school year is extended, greater opportunities will be provided to tailor programs to meet these students' educational needs by the teaching faculty.

Flexibility must be interwoven into the basic organization plan of an extended school year. As already mentioned, teachers' salaries need to be raised to compensate for the extended teaching assignment. There should be a 5-year phase-in period for the extended school year. Parents and teachers must be involved in the process. State legislators need to review the fiscal problems associated with the extended school year at both the local and state levels. Pilot programs need to be studied and evaluated. However, let us not dismiss this proposal without careful study and review.

Now is the time for the educational establishment to assess if the current time frame is meeting our students' needs. So often during the summer months, our children have no place to go. Time is poorly utilized, the cost of a child's attending summer camp for many families is beyond their financial means, and many children and teens go unsupervised because the parents are working, which may (and too often does) lead to gang involvement and serious mischief.

Some school districts have opted for limited, extended pilot programs that include many time configurations. These attempts are a good start in moving this proposal in the right direction. Our schools can ill afford to be bound to a tradition that is as archaic as the horse and buggy. The length of our current school year dates back to the 19th century and early 20th century. The demands of farm life then required children to help with the family chores and perform the numerous responsibilities associated with farming. The economies of the United States and the world have drastically changed since then, and reasons for the current length of the school year no longer exist.

Our school buildings, like the factories of our industrial complex, cannot be allowed to lie idle for a single day, but must be utilized to promote and develop the most important commodity that our nation possesses—the human potential, talent, and intellect of our children. Let us move forward. Research has indicated that schools with extended learning opportunities have increased student academic performance and have made efficient use of the school's physical facilities.

On one hand, parents frequently say, "What am I going to do with my children during the summer months? Our family cannot afford a school tutor or pay for summer camp or employ someone to be with our children." Many children come from homes in which both parents are working or are being raised by one working parent. On the other hand, many teachers enter the summer job market looking for employment opportunities to supplement their family income. Why not employ teachers for the extended school year? The time has arrived for our school culture and history to come to terms with the new educational changes that confront our nation and are necessary to compete in the global economy.

In conclusion, the extended school year provides equal educational opportunities regardless of the socioeconomic status of the student. The extended school year and school day would provide parents with the benefit of having their children supervised by a licensed teacher while being exposed to additional learning and enrichment experiences. Otherwise, many of these students would be on the streets, watching television, and/or participating in other nonproductive activities.

If we are genuinely concerned about lower-income students being unable to afford tutors or lacking parental supervision after school, then citizens should not hesitate to let their voices be heard about this issue. This matter goes beyond just lower-income students. All students would benefit from the extended school year. Teachers should not view the extended school year as a threatening educational innovation that would:

- Reduce their proportional earning power
- Require them to work with a minimal increase in compensation
- Mandate that teachers participate in the extended school year program

KEY QUESTIONS FOR TEACHERS

1. Do you think that an extended school day and school year would improve academic achievement among students?

2. If an extended school day and school year were implemented, do you think criticism about teachers having too much time off would disappear?

3. Many countries have a longer school day and year than do schools in the United States. If we were to imitate them, what effect do you feel it would have on homework, essay writing, and mathematics?

4. What opportunities and benefits could become available to students who attend school for an extended day and year?

5. In your opinion, would the extended school day and school year have a positive effect on how the student spends his or her time?

6. Would you be in favor of an extended school year only for those students who are doing poorly in school?

7. Would you allow students to finish high school in less than 4 years if such students viewed the extended school year as an opportunity for taking extra courses?

8. What about offering more advanced placement courses in high school during the extended school year?

9. Could the extended school year schedule be constructed around the part-time work schedule of students who need to work?

10. What do you think of the extended school year's being a tool to have more limited-ability students finish high school in four years rather than take a longer time?

20

SEPARATE SCHOOLS FOR THE SEXES AND SCHOOL UNIFORMS: ARE OLD IDEAS RETURNING?

Early in our professional lifetimes, we saw single-sex schools and school uniforms as issues of the past. However, the U.S. Department of Education recently issued new rules that will allow schools to offer classes open to students of one sex only and that even permit the existence of single-sex schools. These relaxed restrictions will allow school districts to utilize the single-sex class/school concept as a vehicle to improve students' educational achievement.

In October 2006, the *New York Times* and the *Wall Street Journal* reported that the American Civil Liberties Union (ACLU), the National Organization for Women (NOW), and other groups had denounced these new rules. This was no surprise. On the other hand, it was reported that a coalition of Girl Scouts, a research and advocacy group, and religious educators supported the decision. The Girl Scout coalition pointed out that there was a 24% increase of single-sex classes at 34 private and religious schools over a 10-year period from 1991 to 2001. Almost 70% of the schools in the coalition witnessed increases in single-sex schools.

It is interesting to note that approximately 240 public schools in the United States offer single-sex classes, according to Leonard Sax, a leader in the National Association for Single-Sex Public Education. That is a dramatic increase from the three public schools that offered single-sex classes in 1995.

Informal discussions we had with teachers prior to preparing this chapter indicated that the majority of teachers would welcome single-sex schools and classes, as well as pilot programs to get the issue before the public. They indicated that single-sex schools, at the middle school level, would mitigate problems associated with puberty and diminish distractions between the sexes that resulted in discipline issues. Single-sex schools and classes may result in greater attention being directed to the learning differences associated with sex and age.

There is little doubt that considerable sentiment concurs that single-sex classes and schools should not be limited only to private and religious schools. If the public schools cannot offer vouchers to students so that they can have the choice of which type of school they wish to attend, at least provide these students with the same options already possessed by families who choose to enroll their children in private schools. The political correctness advocates have not recognized that there is strong support and growing popularity for the single-sex school and single-sex classes.

Single-sex public schools were quite common as recently as the late 1950s and 1960s. Then, opponents of such schools complained they were in violation of the Constitution and discriminatory against the excluded gender. Furthermore, numerous so-called research studies surfaced that supported eliminating single-sex schools and classes because doing so would lead to more beneficial social interaction between boys and girls. At best, these research studies presented mixed results and, in the opinion of the authors, were conceived with biased opinions, even before the research was launched.

The authors encourage teachers to examine the many research studies that clearly indicate that boys and girls have different maturity levels and attain different scores across various academic subjects. For example, Carol Gilligan states *In a Different Voice* that girls are different from boys in many respects. Other studies have indicated that girls have a higher academic success rate in elementary schools. Also, girls are more likely than boys to be the teachers' favorites in the elementary grades. The authors have taught in both single-sex and coed schools. It is our view that single-sex schools have many educational advantages over coed schools. This is especially true for grades K–8 and middle schools.

The fact that boys and girls mature at different rates physically, socially, and intellectually is an important reason for considering separation. In middle school and high school, boys and girls become more interested in one another, thus creating a major distraction from the learning process. This, too, is also cited as a reason for separate classes and schools.

Critics of single-sex schools and classes point to the danger that such an approach may result in the same kind of "separate but equal" mentality on gender issues, similar to attitudes that existed in many public schools at the time when children were separated by race. In our opinion, however, this is simply another excuse for opposing the single-sex school concept. The critics have not presented documented evidence as to why single-sex schools should not be established. When the single-sex schools were phased out, approximately 30 to 40 years ago, the data were not there to justify this action. The social and political climate of the time empowered the groups opposing single-sex schools and, with the support of the liberal press and many university professors, they were able to carry the day. Let us not equate racial discrimination with the issue of single-sex schools. They are clearly two separate practices that are worlds apart!

Many educators recognize that research studies have not been conclusive in opposing the single-sex school, yet decades ago many educators jumped on the bandwagon to do away with the single-sex schools and continue today to oppose the new federal guidelines.

The new federal policy mandates that classes or schools that are composed of a single sex must make the same class available to students of both sexes. We have no objection to this mandate, and it is only fair that an option is provided for students to attend coed classes rather than single-sex classes. The authors obviously agree with Education Secretary Margaret Spellings' point that "Every child should receive a high-quality education in America, and every school district deserves the tools to provide it."

Basically, the same groups that oppose single-sex schools also oppose the adoption of school uniforms. The educational establishment is a prisoner to this archaic philosophy that puts restrictions on any endeavor that threatens the beliefs of special interest groups. Many parents today welcome uniforms for their children and are increasingly voicing their support for this policy. For many years, numerous religious groups have conducted separate sex classes and schools and have also mandated the wearing of school uniforms. Why the big fuss? It is about time we revisited old ideas that have worked in the past and apply them today. Of course, these ideas never work perfectly, but they work better than the policies that replace them.

Uniforms contribute to school unity. They also promote school pride and identity. Social class differences in dress are eliminated for all students wearing common uniforms. The authors have not read one research investigation where it has been shown that uniforms have impeded learning. Here again, however, there are segments in our community who associate uniforms with fascism and thus are in violation of democratic principles. We disagree! With violence in our schools being so prevalent, uniforms can contribute to a school climate that diminishes discipline problems and promotes greater student cohesion and respect. Uniforms also eliminate such issues as an acceptable dress code for students attending a school.

In the last analysis, learning and teaching would be helped by single-sex schools and classes and the wearing of student uniforms. They would be a plus in the learning and teaching process. Do uniforms hinder learning at West Point or at the other service academies? In New York City, some Catholic schools require uniforms, and many students attend single-sex schools. Test results demonstrate that children attending these schools score higher on achievement tests than do students in public schools where neither uniforms nor single-sex schools and classes exist. Therefore, those who oppose returning to the traditional single-sex school or classes and uniforms have no rationale for their position other than their marriage to a social philosophy that reminds one of political correctness.

KEY QUESTIONS FOR TEACHERS

1. How effective do you think a single-sex school would be in meeting the needs of adolescents?
2. What is the effect of single-sex education on children? Is it "true life"?

3. Why have most colleges moved to coed schooling? Is the environment in colleges comparable to that of public schools?

4. Do you think that having students separated by gender will create a better learning environment?

5. Is a policy on uniforms or single-sex schools related to learning?

6. Do you think it would be easier for you to teach if all the students wore uniforms and were in a single-sex school?

7. Do you think wearing a uniform in school changes behavior?

8. Should a policy regarding the wearing of uniforms be set by the school authorities or by the community?

9. Why do many individuals oppose the concept of mandating school uniforms and the existence of single-sex schools?

10. Can such critics be convinced that their views may not be beneficial to children?

㉑

TEACHER BURNOUT: MYTH OR REALITY?

As we have stated more than once, the classroom teacher has an extraordinarily difficult job. It is interesting that some critics claim that teaching is an easy profession and that teachers have limited responsibilities. They point to the teachers' work schedule of 180 days and the usual school day ending between 2:30 P.M. and 3:30 P.M. Those of us who have taught know that this assumption is false and that such critics do not have an understanding or knowledge of the demands placed on teachers.

Teaching is an extremely taxing occupation that can be emotionally, physically, and psychologically consuming. Teachers often have their students in mind and heart 100% of the time. Not a day goes by in which student problems are not in the forefront of the teacher's thoughts. For many teachers, the school bell is ringing 24 hours a day.

The end of the school day does not necessarily relieve the teacher from musing over the day's activities and planning future learning and teaching strategies. Lesson plans need frequent review and revisions. Grading student homework requires the teacher to promptly return assignments with commentary. When necessary, teachers need to communicate with working parents after school hours. This person-to-person contact is very much part of the fabric of the teacher's role. The "ivory tower" is frequently mentioned when education is discussed. In reality, however, no moat divides the schoolhouse from parents, students, and the community.

The authors recall that when they started their teaching careers they were exhausted at the end of the school day and usually fell asleep in a matter of seconds after arriving home. We were young men in our 20s and in excellent health. Nevertheless, the psychological stress of teaching drained us of our energy. No professional training we received prepared us to overcome the multitude of pressures that we faced in front of a class of 30 to 35 students.

Our parents were immigrants and held menial, low-paying jobs that required long hours away from home. They were astonished to find their sons sound asleep when they returned from work. They simply could not understand why these young men were so tired from teaching. After all, teaching was a nice "white-collar" job with short hours. The authors' parents were no different from millions of other Americans who found it difficult to comprehend the "burnout" problems facing teachers. Regrettably, it is not surprising that the American public does not fully grasp the manifestations of this issue.

Burnout, as defined in *Webster's New Collegiate Dictionary* and in *Roget's II: The New Thesaurus*, is to "break, to lose energy and strength, to become ineffective, to give out, to become tired and to be in a state of emotional or mental turmoil." Burnout does fit many of these definitions, but teacher burnout goes beyond these traditional definitions and has broader implications.

The school is a very complicated social institution, and it is one that has drastically changed over the past several decades. Enormous pressures are placed on the teachers' shoulders—such as the pressures from increased testing, greater emphasis on accountability issues, and the teaching of controversial subjects—that are dividing the faculty, administration, students, and community. The attacks on teachers by students, student-on-student crimes, and classroom discipline problems also make teaching even more difficult. The pressure gauge has been escalating, and teachers are worried about their safety and their ability to be effective in this conflict-surrounded environment.

In response to these pressures, many teachers are leaving the profession, transferring to suburban schools, accepting teaching positions in private and religious schools, or requesting sick leave, sabbaticals, or assignments outside of the classroom. Teacher attitudes, philosophical views, economic considerations, and professional job responsibilities are associated with continuous pressure to increase pupil achievement. Coupled with job opportunities now available outside teaching, many teachers are leaving the field. Burnout, however, is a relative term, one that is difficult to understand. Teacher burnout may be the most important factor in this ongoing exodus.

It is not easy to discern the symptoms of teacher burnout. For example, these symptoms can also apply to teachers who are very successful in the classroom, spend their entire career in the classroom, and manage to stay on the job regardless of experiencing some form of teacher burnout. Medical experts and career counselors often point to symptoms that may be reflected in many other diseases, as well as being applicable to burnout. One can cover the medical gamut attempting to analyze indications of burnout. The authors have noted such symptoms as headaches, excessive absences, lack of punctuality, alcohol and/or drug use, poor lesson preparation, hostility toward students, lack of energy, and loss of self-confidence and self-esteem as possible indicators of teacher burnout. Each person handles stress and medical problems differently. Attitudes are a very personal matter, and the high stakes that now confront our teachers make burnout an issue that can no longer be ignored.

Loneliness is usually associated with depression and other psychological disorders. However, strange as it might sound to the general public, many teachers fall victim to loneliness during the school day. All adults seek companionship and socialization; however, a teacher's contact with adults during the school day is often limited and usually confined to the lunch hour, hall duty, and, in some schools, teacher preparation periods.

Teachers sometimes find that spending 5 to 6 hours a day with young children and teens does not fulfill their craving for fellowship and adult interaction. Teachers frequently become restless, bored, lose focus, lack stimulation, and look forward to the school day coming to an end. These symptoms, research tells us, may play an important role in causing a chemical imbalance and contributing to the teacher's becoming ineffective and psychologically removed from the classroom. Teaching is a hands-on profession, and it is paramount that the teacher is mentally engaged in classroom activities.

It follows that if burnout is applicable to the teaching profession, why should it not be a factor in other professions or occupations? For example, in other professions and occupations, persons usually are able to remove themselves from the situation and "collect their thoughts." There are very few professions/occupations where a person cannot find time to relax for a moment. Teachers, however, must be alert every minute and provide direction and leadership to the children in the classroom. Think of a teacher as being "on-stage" for over 6 hours per day, day after day. Then think how difficult it would be for an actor or an actress to perform on stage day after day, for 6 hours a night.

MENTAL HEALTH BURNOUT CHECKLIST FOR THE CLASSROOM TEACHER

- Are you fearful or do you have anxiety concerns regarding your students, parents, and colleagues?
- Do you feel you have lost your self-esteem?
- Do you have headaches, or are you unable to sleep?
- Do you constantly worry about your job?
- Are you eating healthy meals?
- Are you happy with your teaching assignment?
- Do you like your pupils?
- Do you have hostile feelings toward administrators, parents, and your students?
- Do you feel inhibited when interacting with your peers?
- Have you noticed a change in your behavior?
- Are you satisfied that you selected teaching as a career?
- Do you feel lonely in the classroom?
- Do you find yourself exhausted at the end of the school day?
- Have you had a recent medical check-up?

- Do you exercise frequently?
- Are you seeking a career change?
- Are you nervous when you see the principal?
- Do you hate going to work in the morning?
- Can you sleep well at night thinking of your next day at school?
- Do you have chaos in your personal life?
- Have you noticed that your enthusiasm for teaching has decreased?
- How are you getting along with friends and family?
- Do you feel you are constantly stressed?
- Are you bored with your work?
- Do you feel as if the school day never ends?
- Do you feel that you are assigned too many classes?
- When your students do not grasp the major points in your lesson, do you become demoralized and give up?

This simple mental health checklist may serve as a guide for the teacher. Seeing the family doctor or counselor is an important first step in dealing with this issue. Counseling may alleviate burnout symptoms in the early stages. Remember, a person's thoughts can lead to cognitive perception distortions and personality disorders.

Teacher training institutions, school boards, superintendents, and principals need to recognize possible burnout symptoms and provide (1) psychological counseling; (2) mental health, nutrition, and intervention classes; and (3) encourage more free time for social interaction among teachers during the workday.

There is no doubt that the status of the profession, as cited in chapter 1 of this book, is not a positive force in combating teacher burnout. There is a need to build positive teacher attitudes and perceptions about themselves and their profession. We need to revitalize our teaching staffs and upgrade the professional status of teachers. In addition, there is a need to reduce K–12 teaching loads so they are comparable to professors' teaching in community and 4-year undergraduate programs. Teachers, like their professional colleagues in higher education, require private offices to meet parents and students. They also need a place to reflect, to enjoy quiet time, and to attend to classroom assignments and related responsibilities. Burnout is by no means a myth. Rather, it is a reality facing the teaching profession.

KEY QUESTIONS FOR TEACHERS

1. What is your feeling regarding the concept of teacher burnout?
2. Do you think a teaching schedule similar to that of the college professors can ever be a reality for teachers?
3. Do you feel you are able to tolerate behaviors of your students better now than when you first started to teach?
4. Would it be of help to have teachers change the grade level and class assignments from year to year?
5. What could you do to vary the activities of content in your courses to ensure that you are not burning out?
6. What are your greatest fears in your teaching day?
7. Do you "take home" many of your school-day problems? If so, what do you do about them?
8. Have you had any discussions in your teacher preparation program for handling the problem of burnout?
9. Should a counselor be available in your school to assist teachers?
10. What would you recommend to your school system to help prevent teacher burnout?

22

SCHOOL SAFETY AND VIOLENCE: IS THERE A SOLUTION?

More than 30 years ago, Vairo and Marcus wrote an article dealing with violence in our secondary schools. For the most part, the research focused mainly on gang violence and student-on-student crimes. There was no way for us, however, to anticipate that 30 years later, violence would be so prevalent that it would extend from the elementary grades into our universities and would be directed so frequently at teachers.

Not a day passes that the various media fail to report stories on violent crimes taking place in our schools. Violence is not limited to our own country. Reports of cases of physical abuse of teachers and harassment are on the increase throughout the world. The British Broadcasting Corporation (BBC) recently reported that violent attacks on teachers by students are taking place at the rate of one a day. More than 85,000 teachers have experienced some kind of aggressive behavior during the past several years.

It is evident that violence in our schools, particularly against teachers, is becoming a worldwide problem. Countries across the globe find that violence against teachers is escalating at a rapid rate. Countries like Scotland, England, Zimbabwe, South Africa, and Malta, just to name a few, say that their teachers are experiencing more student attacks than ever before.

In the United States, the tragic killings at Columbine High School in Colorado and the massacre at Virginia Tech certainly brought the issue of violence to the forefront of the general public and the educational community. Recently, stories have been reported in the press about teachers who were attacked by a fifth-grader and a second-grader in separate incidents. Studies in Illinois and Missouri revealed that violence permeates all grades. A student in Philadelphia, for example, kicked a pregnant teacher. In New York City, it was reported that desks are thrown at teachers, and teachers have been physically attacked. In Florida, a student shot his teacher. The stories go on and on about violence in our schools. It is interesting and disturbing to note that violence is surfacing in all geographical parts of our country—in rural and suburban areas as well as our metropolitan centers. In California, crimes against students and educators in schools have nearly doubled over a 6-year period.

Terrorist groups around the world further complicate the issue of improving safety. Several years ago we saw an attack on a Russian school and the slaughter of students and teachers. Terrorists can and may very well penetrate our schools. The global community can no longer be complacent about school safety. The authors do not want to convey the impression that they are overly alarmist, but our society cannot ignore this tragic crisis.

Teachers must be educated relative to those early warning signals that are exhibited by students who may be prone to excessive violent behavior. These clues are basic and need to be part of the teacher's survival kit. Teachers, along with counselors, psychologists, social workers, and parents, must be aware that a child's history of violence and aggressive behavior cannot be ignored. Children with drug or alcohol abuse issues should be referred to appropriate school personnel for follow-up actions. Poor academic achievement, a poor attendance record, and lateness are also benchmarks of potential trouble. Classroom outbursts and anger need to be closely monitored. Behavior at home that appears to be suspicious needs to be reported. All or any one of these signals may be contributing factors in the violent behavior of the student. Also, our courts, school administrators, and parents have often ignored bullying, physically abusive behavior, and other verbal and nonverbal signs that reflect aggressive behavior.

School districts need to develop a violence prevention program. In 2000, then-Governor Pataki of New York signed into law the Safe Schools Against Violence in Education Act. This legislation provided teachers and administrators opportunities to be involved and to participate in the development of school district policies to protect the welfare of students and the professional staff.

The bill had many positive components that provided for developing safe schools in New York. The legislation is not a cure-all for violence but, in the authors' opinion, it is a step in the right direction. The bill provided penalties for violent crimes perpetrated on the professional staff. Teachers were given the authority to remove disruptive students from their classes. School districts are required to adopt a code of conduct. All school personnel are required to undergo a legal background check. Teachers and other professional staff are required to complete course work in school violence and prevention. The above are only some of the provisions of the bill. Teachers need a safe and secure environment.

All violence prevention plans need to include the early warning signs of potentially violent behavior, which the authors addressed earlier in this chapter. The plan needs to include referral procedures so that students may receive professional help. Assistance should never be delayed, and must involve the appropriate professional personnel. The police department should always be included. Frequently, the police may be the last to be informed and, at times, they may even be omitted from the process. School districts in the past frequently wished to keep violent incidents quiet and, therefore, avoid press coverage that would shed a negative light on the district. This practice is a mistake. Police should be called whenever there is a situation involving violent, physical actions.

If we are going to make progress in this area, teachers must be involved in developing the guidelines and receiving the necessary training to handle behavior problems. The school must have an overall plan for school disruptions. Students, too, must be involved and educated in the problems associated with behavioral issues. The schools are no longer safe havens for students or teachers.

A word or two about bullying: This issue has been and will continue to be a serious problem in our schools. It can no longer be ignored. School personnel must be proactive in preventing bullying and taking corrective action to either remove the offending student from the school or class or, when appropriate, suspend that student from school. Whatever action is taken, professional help must be provided. Teachers must report bullying to the school psychologist and/or school counselor. Early signs of bullying must be reported. For much too long, innocent children have suffered physical and verbal abuse from their bullying peers.

Compulsory attendance laws, as they are now constituted and expressed, work on the underlying assumption that students staying in school will want to learn and become good citizens. On the other hand, one can readily raise the issue: Is school for everyone? Why must we spend millions of dollars enforcing compulsory attendance laws? Students who are forced to stay in school against their wishes become bullies, troublemakers, and hard-core disciplinary cases. So, what is the alternative?

That is the troubling question facing our society. If given the opportunity to go to work in state-sponsored jobs, would these students accept going to work? Furthermore, the only type of work they probably could do would be jobs that required little skill and responsibility. Although most students who quit school after reaching the compulsory attendance age do not fare well in the job market, should we continue to keep students in school if they do not wish to attend and are below the mandatory age to leave school legally?

This is a complex issue but, when millions of dollars are spent on enforcing state school attendance laws, hard questions need to be asked and then addressed. Schools cannot be battlegrounds for students who bring knives, guns, and other weapons to school and disturb classroom instruction. Frequently, parents, teachers, counselors, and administrators have been surprised because they missed early signs of violence displayed by a student. We do not have absolute answers. Nevertheless, school professionals and parents must be diligent partners in the early identification, treatment, and prevention of violence among students prone to such behavior in our schools.

School districts need to increase their safety patrols and promptly suspend high behavior-risk students from their schoolhouse upon commission of a violent act. School districts today have had ample warnings and can no longer be surprised at the violent crimes committed or inadequate safety regulations in force in some schools. Parents, too, must accept responsibility for their children's actions and not be in denial. The whole community must address this issue.

Drinking and drug use are contributing factors to violence in our schools. Therefore, random drug testing of students has become routine for many middle school and high school students, especially for those involved in athletic programs and extracurricular activities. It has been estimated by the White House Drug Policy Office that approximately 2,000 public and private school districts conduct some form of drug testing. The National School Boards Association recently reported that 5% of the public school districts test athletes and 2% test students who are involved in other extracurricular activities. It seems that our large-city school districts and predominantly urban districts have shown some hesitation about establishing drug testing programs. The authors clearly recognize the concern for individual privacy, but this issue goes beyond privacy. Health and safety concerns should be the foremost considerations.

STUDENT BEHAVIOR WARNING SIGNS

- Suicide attempts
- Physical attacks on others or self-mutilation
- Withdrawn behavior
- Attracted to violent literature
- Personal writings contain considerable violence
- Frequently displays enraged behavior
- Relationship with gangs
- Strong feelings of prejudice
- Abuses animals
- Expresses hostility to fellow students
- Consistently disruptive in class
- Ignores teacher's commands
- Leaves school without permission
- Refuses to do homework
- Comes to school intoxicated
- Spends inordinate time on a computer playing violent video games

Recently, a wave of molestation incidents have been reported in which teachers have committed sexual crimes against students. This has been particularly troubling, for even elementary and middle-school children have been involved. These incidents have included both male and female educators and students.

The *New York Times* reported that President Bush convened a School Safety Summit on October 11, 2006, at which Attorney General Alberto Gonzales discussed the urgent need to ensure that American children are safe in the schoolhouse and in their communities. All too regularly, media have been reporting such acts as sexual abuse and molestation allegations against teachers charged with seducing their students, students imitating the Columbine shooters or the Amish country killings, and students receiving severe injuries at the hands of school bullies. Safety issues now extend beyond protecting students from other students. We must now also be concerned with nonstudent intruders entering the school, students physically attacking teachers, and teachers molesting students.

Regulations must be implemented in our schools to protect students from teachers and other school employees. When sexual predators work inside the schoolhouse, the very fabric of American education is threatened. We cannot tolerate such behavior, and the educational establishment and our courts must act swiftly to protect our children.

During the past several decades, public opinion polls, such as the annual Gallup Poll, have indicated that the lack of discipline and the increase in violence are viewed as the most serious problems facing American education. One cannot have learning and teaching when lack of discipline and violence become the number one concerns for teachers, parents, and students. If violence in our schools is not halted, we shall witness a collapse of the American educational system.

Obviously, there is no way society can protect every child from every assault, every bully, and every threat. However, what happened in Lancaster County, Pennsylvania, where the Amish community is located and where crime is almost nonexistent, indeed raised eyebrows. The recent murderous rampage by one student at Virginia Tech illustrates how violence has spread to our universities. The authors believe that strong antiviolence workshops, codes and enforcement of school disciplinary procedures, and even the appointment of a security officer to most K–12 schools would be an appropriate response in the face of such tragedies.

Reports point out that the statistical data are alarming when one considers that nearly 17,000 students per month receive injuries from violent acts on the school premises. Additionally, approximately two million students are suspended from school annually for a variety of misbehaviors, ranging from minor incidents to felony convictions.

Even under the best of circumstances, lack of discipline rears its ugly head in our schools and classrooms. Nevertheless, the authors wish to reiterate that teachers and school administrators need to follow effective disciplinary practices that may contain and/or alleviate the disciplinary problems. They are:

- Be specific in explaining rules and regulations to students.
- Enact behavior codes that are practical and enforceable.
- Limit the number of rules, but make them clear and understandable to the age group you are teaching.
- Be consistent in responses to student behavior.
- Provide reasonable punishment.
- Corporal punishment is not recommended.
- A schoolwide plan needs to be developed to address violence and disciplinary problems, and to generally promote safety in the school.
- More effective sharing of information on potentially violent students is a must, even if this is done at the expense of some individual rights of privacy.

Once the strategies are developed to handle violence, sexual abuses, and disciplinary problems, and these policies are formalized, they must be communicated to teachers, supporting staff, students, parents, the general community, and the local police department. The latter should be an active partner in addressing school safety issues and severe disciplinary problems. Even if a school can develop excellent policies, these policies can become "paper tigers" if the school administration neglects to provide training programs, periodic evaluation meetings, new techniques and strategies to meet new challenges, and continuous feedback to update and modify such existing policies.

When reviewing school safety and disciplinary problems, one cannot escape the issues related to child-rearing and values. It seems our society has become permissive, and children see many gray areas of behavior. Also, the communications world has replaced the parent as the model, and it has introduced many unacceptable examples to children, even in their own homes. It is not surprising that role conflicts and contradictions are factors contributing to these issues surrounding our schools today. The question the authors frequently ask is "What social institutions are providing model behavior attributes for your young?" Furthermore, there is a value conflict ongoing in our society that complicates codes of behavior often accepted by schools, parents, students, and the community.

Questions are also being asked, such as "Should not the federal government be called upon to keep our children safe?" It seems that our local and state police departments have been unable to control violence in our schools. Also, in many instances, school authorities have been historically reluctant to involve law enforcement authorities to investigate violence in the schools. The authors contend that the local police authorities do not have enough staff to adequately address these issues. A broad, systematic approach is needed, and stringent rules must be implemented and enforced in every school in our land.

As the authors were concluding this chapter, a special bulletin was relayed on television that a student in East Orange County, Florida, was stabbed at a bus stop in front of his middle school. Violence needs to be curtailed in our schools, and now is the time for all of us to act.

KEY QUESTIONS FOR TEACHERS

1. To what extent do you feel school violence is caused by schools?
2. What teacher actions facilitate school violence?
3. How can parent involvement help diminish school violence and disciplinary problems?
4. Will laws against school violence alone help?
5. What are some of the warning signs of potential violent behavior?
6. How can a total school effort alleviate violent behavior?
7. What are some behaviors of teachers that, in your opinion, should not be tolerated?
8. What behaviors of children or teachers must be reported to authorities?
9. How involved should the community at large be with school violence and serious disciplinary problems?
10. Should schools that experience a great deal of violence be guarded by the local police department?

23

THE MIDDLE SCHOOL: IS IT EFFECTIVE?

As aspiring teachers attending college, the authors recall reading about how excited many educators were with the introduction of the junior high school organization into school systems across our nation. It was thought that this new school unit would be the panacea for the educational problems and shortcomings that had arisen among children attending schools organized from kindergarten through the eighth grade and again among students attending grades 9–12 high schools. Until the late 1930s and 1940s, students generally spent 8 years in elementary school and 4 years in high school. This was commonly known as the 8-4 system. Supporters of the junior high school system believed that, by introducing a new type of school containing grades 7–9, that this would lead to greater curriculum flexibility and more age-appropriate behavior among students. Thus, the 6-3-3 system of school organization came to replace the 8-4 organizational system.

Supporters of this new organizational structure complained that perennialists and essentialists, who were advocates of traditional education, were responsible for delaying the implementation of this so-called progressive, innovative idea. They believed that rearranging the structural organization and combining a more cohesive age-related and psychologically balanced student body (grades 7–9) would facilitate learning and teaching.

The critics of this new educational unit pointed out that it was not cost effective and that the proposed curriculum would not enhance the mastery of the three R's and basic subject matter content. The authors concur with this conclusion. The emphasis that was placed on socialization did not prove to be a positive vehicle for educational achievement. The creation of the junior high school unit not only complicated student behavioral problems but, as a result, teachers did not want to be assigned to these schools or teach in these difficult circumstances. In school districts like New York City, teachers who did not pass the more rigorous high school examination applied for a junior high school teaching position. It was usually not a desirable assignment.

Teaching in junior high served as a stepping-stone for beginning teachers and those who failed to obtain a high school position. The status of junior high school teachers was never equal to that of high school teachers and, for many years, the salaries were not equal. Catholic schools, other religious-affiliated K–8 grade schools, and elite private schools did not join the bandwagon. Unlike public educators who were not as sensitive to capital construction costs and the duplication of services and materials, the private sector was well aware of the costs and did not believe the change was justified based upon both economic and educational considerations. They proved to be right! We have the same problem today. Money is expended, and the results do not substantiate the burden that is placed on the taxpayer. Structural changes in the organization of schools do not translate into better education for students. Such organizational changes simply hide the failure to adequately educate our students. It gives the *impression* of change—that something is being done to improve education. This is nonsense!

Accountability was completely ignored and not applied when the advocates of the junior high school were in positions of power. We often ask our students to be diligent in doing their class assignments and homework. The same question should have been addressed to our school leaders. Too often in education, cursory research—which may be biased, opinionated, or faulty in design—is accepted as the infallible truth and becomes the basis for decision making. Also, the authors have found some instances in which conclusions are established before data are collected in order, substantiating these conclusions only as an afterthought.

After five or six decades of the existence of the junior high school, educators introduced the middle school concept, yet another supposed answer to facilitate the educational process. Many school districts now reorganized schools by separating students into grades K–4, 5–8, and 9–12. It appears to the authors that the profession has a road map that is directed without stop signs or clear signals. The American public has for too long heard rhetoric, recommendations, and proposed solutions that have confused and mystified not only the general public but rank-and-file teachers as well. Over the decades, new educational vocabulary has been introduced but, in the authors' view, these are old ideas with a new name or twist. In the last analysis, the result is that the "solutions" they promise tend to be just propaganda.

It must be pointed out that the educational establishment believes that changing the school structure will solve our educational problems. Every 20 years or so, a new structural plan has been introduced. The real issue is not the organizational structure. The jargon used in educational circles should be viewed with great suspicion. All of us have heard of such terms as decentralization, centralization, new math, whole language, charter schools, magnet schools, behavioral objectives, and student portfolios, to list just a few examples. Many texts are on the market whose authors are heralded as educational messiahs or educators of great vision. As one progresses in life, it soon becomes apparent that there are no quick solutions to complex issues. Education proposals recommending change need careful study and investigation. It only follows that the authors' concerns apply equally to the middle school as to the junior high. We saw the great hopes many educators had for the junior high schools fail to materialize. We now question if the middle school is an effective delivery agent of quality education.

If the truth be told, one would be hard-pressed to observe tangible, concrete differences between the middle school and the junior high school. We thus raise the following questions:

- Where is the research comparing the relative success of the middle school as opposed to the junior high school? Why the change in school organization?
- Let us go a step further. How did students who completed the traditional 8-4 school organization compare to students who now complete

systems reorganized into K–4, 5–8, and 9–12 schools? (We believe that the students attending the 8-4 schools outperformed our present students.)

- What are the cost differences between operating 8-4 schools and school systems organized to include a middle school? Are costs are much higher for three units, as opposed to two structures?
- Are there really any different certification requirements among teachers in elementary, middle, and high schools?
- Were teachers less effective in the 8-4 organizational structure? (In our opinion, they were more effective.)
- If the middle school organization provides special programs and meets individual students, would it make sense to move to a 3-3-3-3 organizational structure?
- Should elementary schools cease to be organized by grade, as advocated by Goodlad and Anderson in their book *The Non-Graded Elementary School*?
- Are there any substantive content differences between middle and charter schools? (Other than administrative and budget procedures, in reality, there are very few, if any differences.)

Despite the rationale that the educational establishment has provided the general public for these various school organization units, the reliability and validity of the data are questionable. Further, whether we are dealing with a junior high school, a middle school, a charter school, an academy, or a magnet school, today's students are not achieving any better and in many cases far below the performance of students who attended the 8-4 traditional schools. We note that the school dropout rate is higher than ever. Functional illiterates are graduating from our schools at all levels. We are spending more money on education than any other country in the world, yet we rank lower than many other industrialized nations in terms of student achievement. Disciplinary problems, crime, and violence are escalating in our middle and high schools, regardless of the organizational structure.

Let us get back to basics. Regardless of the school unit organization, it is the classroom teacher who will make the difference in the learning process. We doubt very seriously that teachers have been consulted as the student articulation flow shifted from (1) elementary school to high school; (2) elementary school to junior high school to high school; (3) elementary school to middle school to high school; (4) elementary school to charter school to high school; (5) elementary school to magnet school to high school; (6) elementary school to academy to high school; and (7) to other so-called innovations that may be on the drawing board.

We should not abandon our desire to explore a variety of educational configurations, but we need to take precautions because we cannot drift from one school organization to another without careful study.

Finally, the authors do not believe the key to learning lies in the school organization of grades. Good, dedicated teachers are the essential ingredient for effective learning and a sound education. Today the educational establishment is returning to the 4-year high school that was conceptually abandoned four decades ago. Educators need to keep their eyes on the ball. The primary order of business is promoting an educational environment that ensures that each student counts and is not a number.

Jane Brody, in a very provocative article entitled *Help for the Child Who Says No to School,* which appeared in the *New York Times* on August 26, 2006, pointed out that children who move from the elementary school and are thrust into the chaotic middle school often develop psycho-social problems. The transition to middle school for many students may contribute to the crises in self-confidence and self-esteem. The ages of 10 to 13 are difficult years, and the large impersonal middle school may not be the answer. Combining students in this age group can prove to be an explosive counterforce to learning and teaching. Yet today, the middle school is the new star for solving the educational problems confronting children 10 to 13 years of age.

Let us focus on promoting the best interests of students rather than spend decades proposing school unit structures and spending tax dollars that in the last analysis have not proven to be the answer to our educational problems. Over the years, the authors have discussed school organization with graduate students, parents, principals, and teachers. There was no clear understanding among any of these groups of the various unit organizations that were discussed in this chapter. The authors were not surprised by this feedback, for they, too, do not grasp the significance of the different organizations that have emerged. Additionally, school principals expressed mixed feelings to the authors about the various unit structures. Therefore, why is all this energy wasted on school organization?

KEY QUESTIONS FOR TEACHERS

1. In what ways did the curriculum change when the 8-4 system was changed to the 6-3-3 system and then to the 5-3-4 system?
2. Is it possible that separate schools for elementary children and high school students are not the solution?
3. What do you think are the pros and cons of the middle school concept?
4. How related should the curriculum of the middle school be to the high school?
5. What are the advantages and disadvantages of charter schools and public schools?
6. Does the organization of the school have an effect on learning?
7. If the decision was yours, what type of school organization would you recommend?
8. Are schools spending too much time worrying about the mental adjustment of their students?
9. To what extent is the organization of schools a problem to the school system? To the community? To the teaching profession?
10. What differences in curriculum are there between an 8-4 and a 5-3-4 organization?

(24)

POLITICAL AND SOCIAL ACTIVISM IN THE SCHOOL: WHAT ARE THE PROS AND CONS?

Research indicates that the past 10 years have been a decade of increased student political and social activism in our schools. This really is not surprising, inasmuch as our society has become so polarized on so many issues that ideological conflicts are common, not only in the United States but elsewhere in the world.

Youth organizations around the world are focusing on government-related problems, as well as social issues. Their membership has increased, and their issues cover the political spectrum. The once-held belief among students that their voices were not heard and that they really did not matter is evaporating, and many now feel that they are no longer restricted by the old social order.

In the 1950s, concern was expressed that our students were apathetic and indifferent to political and social issues. With the Vietnam War, college students' participation in political and social issues exploded. Today, we are observing another surge among high school students, and even in the lower grades, to actively participate in the debate surrounding the crucial issues facing our society. The core values and beliefs held by Americans are being challenged as well as defended by various segments of our population. American foreign policy and economic positions are also under attack and are no longer as sacrosanct as they once were.

Students are not sitting on the sidelines but are becoming key players in the battleground of ideas. They are joining groups that represent the political and social spectrums in our society. Whether the issue is school prayer, abortion, free speech, sex education, or foreign and domestic economic policies, student political participation and students' voices are being heard throughout our nation.

Students may not only be the real silent majority, but more importantly, they are our future voters and leaders, and are expressing their thoughts now rather than waiting until they are eligible to vote. Complementing student activism is the recognition that our schools must recognize that controversial issues must be included in the school program. Why not? The heart of learning is critical thinking and analytical reasoning. No subject should be excluded as long as it is treated in an objective fashion and its content is age appropriate.

Students are demanding that controversial subjects should be the centerpieces to the learning process. These topics must be vital components of today's school curriculum. The old, traditional notion of citizenship has now become embedded into a broader educational concept. This new philosophical perspective reaches beyond the very basic foundation upon which past generations held to those traditional values and beliefs. Social institutions are changing and adapting to a new era that requires utilizing the scientific method to study social issues.

Increasingly, our nation is seeing political participation by students and teachers through litigation, protests, increased membership in activist organizations, demonstrations, and rallies. Students and teachers are challenging the status quo and clearly are expressing how they feel about world issues. Blind patriotism is no longer accepted by all, and new ways of tackling social and political problems are being introduced by students active in these movements. The American student is now developing political, social, and media skills in communicating ideas and bringing to the forefront a host of pressing issues that for too long have received minimal attention. Animal rights, the environment, disease, poverty, nuclear war, and other issues of current importance are being raised by student activists. There is a need to educate a new generation of critical thinkers. Youth is on the march, and the schoolhouse door must be open to both the critics and the supporters of traditional thought. We all must recognize that the classroom is a legitimate place for social and political engagement and dialogue for the student. Where else should the students go?

Student activism has indeed introduced many positive benefits. They include:

- Students are more aware of the social and political issues facing our society.
- Students are no longer indifferent to the ideological conflicts confronting us.
- Students have obtained the prerequisite skills to gather data about topics or issues and to arrive at scientifically based rational conclusions.
- Students have developed the ability to substantiate positions that they support.
- Students are more cognizant of the avenues open for change and new opportunities in the political arena.
- Students have shown greater interest in participating in classroom discussions dealing with controversial subjects.
- Students recognize that they are important figures in bringing about reform through their activism.
- Students have learned from direct experiences the value of the freedoms given to us in the Bill of Rights.
- Students understand the intricate relationship between the schoolhouse and the issues facing the broader community.
- Students no longer feel that any subject should be off limits for inclusion in the school curriculum.
- Students are more knowledgeable about current events.
- Students see their activism as a catalyst to bring about equality, justice, and opportunity to all citizens, not only here at home but all over the world.
- Students view their activism as a vehicle to bring different perspectives to the public arena and to initiate change.
- Students see that they can play a role in having the pros and cons of a given issue discussed in the forum of public opinion.

Like every issue that confronts us, there are at least two sides. There are those who do not support student activism and who believe that student activism in social and political activities is not beneficial to the common good. The rationale for this position follows:

- Student activists present a negative image to the general public and to other students.
- Student activists reject and do not appreciate our nation's traditional values and beliefs.
- Student activists are unreasonable and hostile to those holding different and contrary positions.
- Student activists are viewed as pawns for liberal causes and power groups.
- Student activists want to change the traditional character of America and are internationalist in outlook.
- Student activists are involved in propaganda and confrontation.
- Student activists want to destroy our democratic system of government.
- Student activists are not tolerant toward people who view our social order differently.
- Student activists threaten the traditional role of the schoolhouse and contribute to the escalation of violence.
- Student activists are usually inextricably tied to left-wing political groups. There are a smaller number of activists in groups representing right-wing points of view.

Whatever else, student activists have raised the temperature of social and ideological conflict in our schools. The American school is also finding itself to be part of the social conscience of our nation. The authors believe that, although both the pros and cons of student activists have merit, the learning and teaching components have benefited from greater student participation. Because of student activism, the educational establishment and the traditional role of teaching have become more complex and tied to contemporary issues.

The evidence appears clear that a compelling case has been made to continue our support of student and teacher activists, provided they do not use violence and they conform to the laws of our nation. A democratic society needs reformers and critical thinkers who wish to improve the American way of life. We have a wonderful opportunity to open the doors and windows for fresh political thought.

The authors cannot conclude this chapter without noting that, as long as student activists simmer in resentment and hostility, they multiply the odds against success. The only forces that can propel this movement are the forces of human understanding, cordial interaction, and tolerance. It is difficult to assess the strengths of any movement when one is overwhelmed with a sour expression and an aggressive, intolerant message. Incendiary allegations only complicate issues and harden positions on both sides. Mainstream America is not going to succumb to these types of tactics, especially from students. The student activists must avoid being the casualties of negative public opinion.

On the other hand, the 55 million students in our schools comprise a formidable future potential voting group in the decades ahead, and our schools must include controversial issues in the curricula. These issues must be treated openly, objectively, and scientifically.

An educated citizenry must be prepared to enter the world of globalization that is coming upon us quickly. Our students must have a world perspective so that our nation will be competitive in the market of ideas and critical thinking. Thomas Friedman pointed out in his book *The World Is Flat* that innovation, critical thinking, and vision must be encouraged in our schools. Our nation cannot afford to have students who follow past practices without critical examination and continuous investigation.

KEY QUESTIONS FOR TEACHERS

1. The question of student political and social activism is a difficult one for the teacher. How would you react to a politically active student who takes a view that the community opposes?
2. Should the school allow students to take an opposite view from the majority of the adult community?
3. If the question of patriotism is paramount, and one student's view is against the majority, should the teacher defend him or her?
4. Do you agree that any or all subjects should be discussed in the classroom?

5. Could you teach democracy in a classroom if certain views are not allowed to be expressed?
6. How would you ensure that the student activists listen to opposing views?
7. Is it possible to be neutral in a discussion of conflicting views? Is a neutral stance the best way for a teacher?
8. How much say should the community have on the political views of the student population?
9. Is it appropriate for a school to sponsor political activities on the part of its students?
10. What is it that students learn when they are politically active?

25

LIBERAL ARTS AND
TEACHER PREPARATION:
FRIENDS OR MORTAL ENEMIES?

At the very outset of this chapter, the authors want to make it clear that it is not expected that all teachers be replicas of the "Renaissance man." However, even though the era of technology and specialization may be upon us, teachers need to acquire the very traits that they value and wish to impart to their students—the love of learning and the ability to think critically.

It is indeed one of the ironies of education that minimal emphasis has been placed on a liberal education in the preparation of teachers. Allan Bloom, in his book *Closing of the American Mind*, criticized America's colleges and universities for sacrificing true learning to what he called "cultural relativism." Bloom was particularly critical of higher education institutions, which he believed had totally surrendered the mission of true learning for the transitory goal of preparing students for careers. Bloom, along with philosophers like Mortimer Adler and E. D. Hirsch, called for a return to the study of the classics and the broad area of the humanities.

Teachers need to see themselves as a community of scholars in pursuit of knowledge, culture, and the heritage of mankind. Teachers cannot view themselves as simply transmitters of basic skills and knowledge. Teachers must be optimistic, enthusiastic, and committed to learning.

These are prerequisite traits for successful teaching. These traits also apply to students. In many of our colleges and universities, the traditional liberal arts disciplines are considered irrelevant or archaic in the world today. The authors believe that many of the traditional classical disciplines may be more relevant than our students, and even professors, recognize.

We need to view the total teacher education program experience as including the broad liberal arts as well as the professional sequence. The authors believe that tolerance and enthusiastic support for these age-old traditional liberal arts concepts are missing in some of our colleges and universities. By no means are the authors forcing the issue to require students to choose between specialization and the liberal arts. We do believe that both need to carry academic weight in the preparation of teachers. The dual problem that manifests itself today is that teachers may not give much consideration to the liberal arts, but, at the same time, they are not really devoted to their academic discipline. From a professional perspective, teachers cannot continue to be transmitters of elementary skills and knowledge but must seek higher goals for themselves in developing professional competence and intellectual growth.

Teachers in grades K–12 are less likely to be active in professional organizations, attend professional meetings in their academic discipline, or serve on national, regional, or statewide committees than their counterparts in universities or colleges. This academic gap needs to be bridged between teachers and professors.

It seems to the authors that teachers need a strong background in the liberal arts as well as in their academic discipline. William Perel, former director of the In-Service Institute for secondary school teachers of mathematics at the University of North Carolina at Charlotte, along with Vairo, one of the authors of this book, examined the applications of teachers who were admitted to the institute. It was found of the 67 teachers admitted to the Institute, 57 described themselves as full-time mathematics teachers—yet not one teacher belonged to the Mathematical Association of America. The cost for membership at the time of the study was only $6.00. What was even more disturbing was that only 13 of these teachers belonged to the National Council of Mathematics, a professional organization specifically designed for them.

It is not surprising that our society awards greater prestige to individuals who are called mathematicians rather than to those who teach mathematics in secondary school. This applies to all disciplines. An individual who views himself or herself as a historian is more likely to gain greater respect than one who calls himself a history teacher. However, regardless of the above-cited examples, if teachers have little knowledge and appreciation of literature, opera, art, philosophy, and other related areas, then our schools need to reexamine the qualifications of those entering the teaching profession.

It seems to the authors that teachers today need broad preparation in the humanities as well as in-depth knowledge and commitment to their academic discipline. Therefore, greater emphasis needs to be placed on both of these areas. Teachers must be devoted to both their disciplines and the liberal arts to achieve excellence. The authors have observed that a genuine dialogue is lacking in our universities and colleges between the liberal arts faculty and faculty in professional schools, including schools of education. Higher education needs to focus on both areas of study. There is simply no substitute for the traditional liberal arts in higher education curriculum. If our teachers are going to be successful leaders, they must have an appreciation of music, fine art, philosophy, literature, foreign languages, classics, mathematics, logic, and other areas of the humanities. These subjects frequently are areas that students try to avoid or seldom select as electives.

The authors can only conclude that our society has to decide what kind of education should be provided in our colleges and universities. Liberal arts and teacher education cannot be foes or mortal academic enemies. Our teachers need both study areas. The issue of whether Bloom's call for a return of the perennialist philosophy of education as the heart of any undergraduate curriculum is open for debate. However, the authors see merit in Bloom's position and also agree with E. D. Hirsch's position that our schools are producing cultural illiterates. Every teacher should read Hirsch's book *Cultural History*. It is a thought-provoking text that raises numerous issues that need to be studied.

There are those who believe that American education has drifted away from the traditional liberal arts and the door is closed to the Renaissance concept. We are inclined to agree with this view.

KEY QUESTIONS FOR TEACHERS

1. Did you enjoy your college courses in the liberal arts?
2. Were the courses offered in the liberal arts challenging?
3. Do you consider yourself a Renaissance person?
4. Do you believe studying the liberal arts made you a better person and teacher?
5. Do you think you have a better understanding of civilization because of your preparation in the liberal arts?
6. Why are many prospective teachers "turned off" by liberal arts courses?
7. Can the liberal arts become more meaningful to you?
8. Do you believe that our programs in colleges and universities are too specialized, especially at the undergraduate level?
9. As a teacher, do you consider yourself a member of a community of scholars?
10. Are you devoted to your academic discipline?

26

SCIENCE AND MATHEMATICS: WHERE ARE THEY?

Our colleges and universities are flooded with students majoring in the social sciences, recreation, physical education, teacher education, and other nonscience/nonmath academic specializations—yet our K–12 schools lack qualified teachers in the sciences and mathematics. Many schools lack updated laboratories, and many elementary schools lack even a modest science classroom. It is not a surprise that our nation is failing to provide the required human pool of necessary science and math majors. Our graduate schools are continually finding that students majoring in the sciences, mathematics, computer science, and engineering are foreign students, a large number coming from Asian countries.

This critical situation is not a new development on the American educational scene. From the days of Sputnik in the late 1950s, it was obvious that America's youth were being exposed to a bankrupt system of promoting sciences and mathematics in our schools. During the past 50 years, the authors found that only a very small percentage of American high school students pursue studies in physics, chemistry, and advanced mathematics. Also, poorer school districts usually have had to rely on teachers who lacked certification in these subjects. These poorer district and urban centers have found it almost impossible to attract science and mathematics teachers. Even community colleges and small private liberal arts colleges have had difficulty recruiting professors in these subjects.

There are thousands of teaching vacancies, and school districts are begging for science and mathematics teachers, even those with temporary or provisional certifications. Recruitment of qualified teachers has become a major issue facing our schools. The authors are indeed far from the first educators to point out this problem. More elementary school teachers must have academic preparation in mathematics and science beyond the six credit hours that are usually required by most states for a teaching license. Departmentalization must be instituted in these critical subject areas, beginning in the second grade.

It seems to the authors that cash incentives must be offered to those who prepare to teach science or mathematics in our schools. The New York City Department of Education is currently striving to meet the shortage of math and science teachers by offering up to a $15,000 housing allowance for individuals who are certified to teach in these areas and are willing to come to New York City. Better facilities must be made available so that students are not exposed to archaic experiments and have the latest technology in their classrooms. Class size must be lowered so that individual attention may be given to each student. Guidance counselors must take a proactive rather than a nondirective counseling role in promoting careers in math and the sciences. The authors have found that very few counselors have a science or mathematics background. Thus, they tend to guide students away from areas about which they know little.

Schools must provide opportunities for students to develop skills and critical thinking in our science laboratories. Many students in our schools receive limited exposure to the sciences. Students need early exposure to understand theorems, inductive reasoning, and logic. Such simple topics in our science classes as velocity, pressure, gases, genes, speed of sound, and germs need to be introduced at an early age in child development. Science needs to be challenging and exciting to the elementary school child. It should be applicable to the child's life experiences, provoke curiosity, and serve as an intrinsic motivator to promote and stimulate learning.

Robert J. Krajewski, in an article entitled "Let's Make Learning Fun in the Classroom," pointed out that frequently teachers cause students to drop out of the learning scene at an early age. He asks, "Do we unwittingly make learning, even at an early age, a drudgery or a chore with which to be contended?" Too often, children associate fun only with activities outside of school. Krajewski states that there is a need to make learning come alive in school through fun experiences and elimination of the same old dull routines.

If we can achieve these goals, science and mathematics may have an opportunity to flourish in the schoolhouse. If this happens, students will benefit throughout their lives, and the United States and its citizens will be better able to compete on the world technology stage.

KEY QUESTIONS FOR TEACHERS

1. Would you favor departmentalization in grades 2–5?
2. Why do you believe many students are not attracted to mathematics and science courses?
3. Should the laws of supply and demand determine the salaries of teachers in different subject areas?
4. How many courses have you taken in mathematics and science in your college career?
5. How do students in your school score on national mathematics and science standardized tests?
6. Are the teachers of mathematics and science in your school fully certified?
7. If you are teaching in an elementary school, do the teachers have adequate preparation in science and mathematics?
8. Are all teachers in your college training program required to take science and mathematics courses? At what level, and how many credits were required?
9. Do you have any recommendations to solve the teacher shortage in mathematics and science?
10. Why do you think our schools are failing in these critical subjects?

27

TIPS FOR TEACHERS: HOW CAN YOU BE AN EFFECTIVE CLASSROOM TEACHER?

This chapter is primarily for beginning teachers, but even for more experienced teachers these suggestions can also serve as reminders of the strategies that should be used for effective classroom performance.

These tips by no means guarantee success, but if they are consistently ignored, the authors have found that success as a teacher can be seriously jeopardized. Therefore, we urge teachers to refer to these guidelines as benchmarks that should be incorporated into their daily school and classroom activities. These tips represent only a few from an exhaustive list of possibilities.

TIPS FOR TEACHERS

- Be enthusiastic about your job.
- Be cooperative with your colleagues and principal.
- Take the initiative in communicating with parents.
- Be sympathetic and understanding of home conditions of your students.
- Be positive with students who are failing or are not achieving at grade level.

- Remember that good teaching requires relentless perseverance and patience.
- Teaching involves careful preparation for each day's lesson.
- An understanding of and empathy for children is an important characteristic of the successful teacher.
- Be poised and calm in crisis situations.
- Dress appropriately. You are a role model.
- Encourage all your students, and provide successful learning experiences for them.
- Recognize that students have different abilities, skills, and interests. Select experiences that capitalize on their strengths and provide enrichment exercises to remedy shortcomings.
- Praise students when warranted.
- Volunteer as a tutor in after-school programs.
- Avoid being political activist in the classroom. It will compromise your professional standing and even may jeopardize your teaching position.
- Teaching controversial subjects requires that students hear all sides of the issue and are afforded an equal opportunity to voice their opinions.
- Avoid reading from your notes in lesson presentations.
- Use pivotal questions to stimulate critical thinking.
- Give opportunities to all the students to participate in class discussions. Do not consistently rely on a small number of students to dominate classroom activities.
- Speak in a clear voice so that all the students can hear you.
- Use a variety of teaching strategies such as debates, oral and written reports, experiments, guest speakers, general discussions, book reviews, and problem-solving exercises.
- Computers are usually part of every child's experience. Utilize this familiarity with computers in your classroom activities.
- Rely on all the data available rather than just scores from standardized tests in assessing students.
- Be aware of your classroom environment. Violence, gang activity, vandalism, and verbal and physical abuse need to be immediately recognized and reported.

- In your classroom establish clear, specific rules and regulations on discipline. Explain to pupils why these procedures are in the best interest of both you and the students.
- Involve students in issues in which they can make age-appropriate decisions.
- Be consistent in enforcing rules and regulations that are school policies or which you have established in the classroom.
- Utilize bulletin boards, a class newsletter, telephone calls, e-mails, and letters to the home as means of opening communication lines with both students and parents.
- Be a good listener and do not interrupt students when they are making a class presentation. Give them time to express themselves.
- Listen attentively to student problems. Do not humiliate them.
- Demonstrate warmth with a smile or kind words to your students.
- Prepare students to understand time management in school as well as after school hours.
- Use homework as a tool to reinforce learning or to introduce a new topic or unit. Do not use homework as a punishment tool.
- Provide homework that will not overwhelm the students but can realistically be handled by them.
- Homework assigned should be reviewed by teachers and promptly returned with comments.
- Homework assignments need to be clear and explicit. Students should be given an opportunity to ask questions about assignments.
- When homework is returned, you should encourage questions from the students.
- A variety of activities and exercises should be included in homework assignments.
- Depending on the grade level, homework should not exceed more than 30 to 50 minutes for elementary school grades, especially the lower grades. In middle or high school, the time required to complete assignments should vary from 1.5 to 2 hours.
- Homework should be very much a part of your lesson plans.
- Identify students who may have special needs, and refer them to specialized school personnel, such as the guidance counselor or school psychologist.

- Do not rule out rote learning. This type of learning needs to be integrated into the knowledge and skill base of subject content.
- Be aware that human diversity and multiculturalism are very much part of the fabric of American democracy.
- Students from all backgrounds need to feel comfortable and welcome in the classroom.
- Know your students' names and get acquainted with them within the first two weeks of class.
- Acknowledge your students outside of class: in the hallway, in the library, school cafeteria, playground, or if you should meet them in a public place.
- Attend after-school sports activities, special evening programs, PTA meetings, student performances, and other school student programs.
- Textbooks need to be carefully reviewed prior to using them in the classroom.
- Be prepared when conducting a conference with a parent. It is incumbent on the teacher to provide a warm setting and to immediately establish a good relationship.
- Student growth and development is a day-by-day, cumulative, enriching experience.
- Recognize that there are no quick or easy answers to learning problems and thus you should avoid getting frustrated or angry at the student.
- Encourage students to tell you what they like or dislike about your teaching. Accept their criticism gracefully.
- Take advantage of district in-service courses.
- Enroll in a graduate degree program at a reputable university.
- Visit other schools and school districts to observe "best practices" used by teachers.
- Attend professional meetings and become a member of a professional organization in your subject or teaching area.
- Read books and educational journals dealing with contemporary educational issues.
- Do not be afraid to admit a mistake.
- Confer with your principal, assistant principal, or department chair if you have unanswered questions.

- If you are a beginning teacher, you may wish to keep a personal log and review its contents every week. Reflect on those success experiences and those difficult incidents that, in the future, you would handle differently.
- The teacher's lounge is a great place to socialize, but always keep in perspective professional ethics and student privacy, and avoid participating in general gossip.
- Give careful consideration to where you wish to teach.
- Explore educational possibilities in all sectors of education: public, private, and religious schools.
- Do not hesitate to inquire about professional advancement opportunities.

Good luck to you!

CONCLUDING REMARKS

The problems facing the teaching profession are difficult to portray because they have so many different manifestations. The need to attempt to initiate a discussion and to write a book on this important subject, while difficult and, at times, frustrating, has also been both a challenging and professionally rewarding experience for the authors. Though much is known and much has been written about teaching, it is hoped that this volume has given the reader additional insights and greater understanding of the various forces and factors that have had a significant influence on the teaching profession.

No other profession in our society has been called upon to serve so many needs, to fulfill the aspirations of so many people, and to provide such a variety of educational as well as human services. At no time in our history has so heavy a burden of responsibility been placed on the teaching profession. Yet, at the same time, the profession has never before been so scrutinized and criticized. This is what motivated the authors to undertake this project. Only with a teaching profession that represents the stamp of excellence can the faith that Americans once had in education continue to be the bedrock of the American dream.

The authors trust that this text dramatized the problems and possible solutions facing the teaching profession. We make no pretense that some of the problems have easy solutions. The authors also recognize that some readers of this book may have the feeling that there are too many obstacles for the profession to overcome and that there is little hope for real change. The authors have indicated their optimism and hope that America is now ready and prepared to elevate the teaching profession in the hierarchal world of work so that outstanding, talented individuals will be attracted to its ranks.

In the September 19, 2006, edition of the *New York Times,* it was reported that Arthur Levine, former president of Teachers College/Columbia University, stated that "Teacher education right now is the Dodge City of education, unruly and chaotic." The authors concur with Levine and believe that the education establishment needs to do what the medical profession undertook 100 years ago. At that time, the Flexner Report, a comprehensive study of the preparation of doctors in our medical schools, led to recommendations to upgrade and reform the medical profession.

People are very concerned about our schools and those assigned to teach our children. The seriousness of the situation is reflected in our media, where not a day goes by without some commentary or story about the teaching profession. The authors of this text have attempted to present positive and constructive changes that need to be implemented immediately. Unless the problems facing the teaching profession are solved, our nation will be headed for great disillusionment. Join the authors in their crusade to avoid this catastrophe. Now is the time to act!

You have now completed reading our book and, hopefully, understand the spirit of our message. We trust that you will weigh the issues and take the requisite steps necessary to help solve the pressing education problems that confront our nation. Progress occurs in small steps—sometimes one step at a time.

Our best wishes to you and our special thanks for taking the time to read our book about the issues facing the teaching profession.

SELF-EVALUATION QUESTIONS

1. Are you happy with your present position?
2. Do you plan to enroll for an advanced degree?
3. Do you wish to teach at a different grade level—for example, elementary school, middle school, high school, community college, college or university?
4. To what section of the country would you like to relocate?
5. Where do you plan to be in 5 or 10 years from today in your career ladder aspirations?
6. How do you feel about where American education is headed?
7. What are the major issues that you face as a teacher?
8. Are you satisfied with the safety procedures that your school has established?
9. Is your compensation adequate?
10. Would you like to see merit pay introduced in your school system?
11. Should outstanding teachers receive salaries comparable to school principals?
12. Do you favor affirmative action in faculty appointments and promotion?
13. Are you satisfied with your supervisor?

14. Do you have adequate time to spend with your own children and/or family while holding your full-time teaching position?
15. Do you hold a second job?
16. How do you spend your summers?
17. At what age do you plan to retire?
18. Will your pension be adequate to meet your family's needs?
19. Do you find teaching more or less challenging today than when you began your teaching career?
20. Do you get bored teaching the same material year after year?
21. Do you have opportunities for professional growth and development?
22. How much time do you spend traveling to your teaching assignment each day?
23. What do you wish to do differently in your career in the years ahead?
24. If you had the chance to change careers, would you consider it?
25. What changes do you recommend for the teaching profession in the decade ahead?
26. Have you published any scholarly papers or research documents?
27. Do you review your lesson plans each semester?
28. Do you make any suggestions to your principal?
29. Are you ever invited to make suggestions as to how to improve your school?
30. Do you consider yourself a professional?
31. Do you think teaching is viewed by the general public as a full-fledged profession?
32. As you complete this self-evaluation checklist, is there anything else you should be asking yourself about your profession?

MISCELLANEOUS NOTES

PART I   THE TEACHING PROFESSION TODAY

[M]aking teaching into a more solid and respected profession involves much more than raising teaching salaries; "it" involves the attitudes past and present of what it means to educate.

—A. M. Robin. "Teaching as a Profession: Historic, Public,
Union and Alternative Perceptions," *Path of Learning*, 2000
(retrieved December 6, 2006, from http://www.pathoflearning.net)

The public sees funding as the major problem; it links pre-school programs to school success to teenage years, and expresses a willingness to invest in pre-school programs.

It is political leadership that has failed, and not the schools.

The U.S. Department of Education commissioned a report and concluded that the traditional public schools outperformed their counterparts in Charter Schools in math and reading. The public schools outperformed the private schools!

—L. C. Rose "Myth, Reality and Failed Leadership,"
Phi Delta Kappan 88 (2006), p. 2

Between 1960 and 1998 the cost of education has risen 200%. During the same time period SAT scores declined 60 points.

—J. Ricocco, "Just Facts—1998," *Education*, December 20, 2005

We expect our teachers to handle teenage pregnancy, substance abuse and the failings of the family. Then we expect them to educate our children.

—J. Scully, chairman, president, and CEO, Apple Computers, Inc.

Ten Educational Trends Shaping School Planning and Design:

1. Lines of prescribed attendance will blur.
2. Schools will be smaller and more neighborhood-oriented.
3. Fewer students per class.
4. Technology will dominate instructional delivery.
5. Typical spaces thought to constitute a school may change.
6. Students and teachers will be organized differently.
7. Students will spend more time in school.
8. Grade configuration will change.
9. Schools will disappear before the end of the 21st century—or will they?
10. Instructional materials will evolve.

—K. R. Stevenson, "Ten Educational Trends Shaping
School Planning and Design," *NCEF*, September 2002

Harvard Professor Richard Elmore charged politicians for making performance-based accountability mean testing, and testing alone.

—The National Center for Fair and Open Testing, 1998
(retrieved September 30, 2006, from
http://www.edu-cyberg.com/teachers/standards2.html)

The NCLB law requires "highly qualified" for each teacher—not a single state has met that deadline.

Inner-city school districts often have more than twice as many uncertified teachers as affluent districts do.

—*New York Times*, July 26, 2006

PART II   THE TEACHER AND THE MARKETPLACE

The success of a merit pay program depends . . . on careful, cooperative planning involving all constituencies that will be affected, so that the resulting plan is affordable, acceptable to teachers and adapted to distinct needs.

—T. I. Ellis, "Merit Pay for Teachers,"
ERIC Clearinghouse on Educational Management, 1984

One-third of United States high school seniors can read proficiently. One-quarter of United States high school seniors can barely read at all. Eighty percent are not proficient in math.

—J. Ricocco, "Just Facts–1998," *Education*, December 20, 2005

Education schools and education departments have been called the "intellectual slums" of the university. Whether measured by SAT, ACT vocabulary tests or GRE, students majoring in education have consistently scored below average.

—T. Sowell, "Inside American Education," *Free Press*, 1993

In most professions, the best workers usually receive the top pay—a situation that [was] once held in teaching, before unions arrived . . . and began to demand lockstep salaries . . . frustrated by the absence of reward for ability in public schools, [teachers] have looked elsewhere for more rewarding career paths.

—N. Gelinas, "Time for Merit Pay for Teachers,"
New York Sun, June 20, 2005, p. 9

Teacher quality, as measured by scores on licensing exams and levels of education, shows to be the single strongest predictor of how a child will fare in schools.

—R. Ferguson, Harvard researcher, *Chicago-Sun Times*
(retrieved September 30, 2006,
from http://www.edu-cyberg/com/teaching/standards2.html)

If a teacher only teaches in one way, then they conclude that the kids who can't learn well that way don't have the ability, when, in fact, it may be the way the teacher's teaching that is not a good match to the way those kids learn. And if the teacher tried another way of teaching s/he might find that a lot of kids who now seem dumb really are able to learn the material.

—R. Steinberg, Secrets of the SAT Interviews,
website copyright 1995–2006, WGBB Educational Foundation
(retrieved from www.pbs.org/wgbh/pages/frontline/
shows/sats/interviews/Sternberg.html)

PART III　EFFECTIVE LEARNING AND TEACHING

While blaming the achievement gap on non-school factors, the public believes it is the public schools that close it.

Students in traditional public schools were outperforming their counterparts in charter schools in math and reading.

The public school students outperform their counterparts in private schools.

—L. C. Rose "Myth, Reality and Failed Leadership,"
Phi Delta Kappan, 88 (2006), p. 2

Demographic studies produced by standardized testing companies suggest that well over half the minority/low-income populations would be rejected by [high-level jobs] various screening tests.

—D. Wakefield, "Taking Hope Out of Teaching,"
Phi Delta Kappan, 88 (2006), pp. 79–82

One can imagine the difficulties in teaching a class when there is no discipline. From times in the past to the present time, teachers have had to contend with all kinds of undesirable behaviors which disturb the learning environment.

The annual Gallup Poll of Public Attitudes towards the public last listed "lack of discipline" as the most serious problem facing the education system. *The Harvard Education Letter* (1987) lists such problems as cheating, insubordination and classroom disruptions which lead to nearly 2 million suspensions per year.

You're not going to get anything different if you're not going to do anything differently.

—B. Wheelan, Commission on Colleges,
Southern Association of Colleges and Schools

Tests enhance later retention more than additional study of the material, even when tests are given without feedback. This surprising phenomenon is called the testing effect, and although it has been studied by cognitive psychologists sporadically over the years, today there is a renewed effort to learn why testing is effective and to apply testing in educational settings.

—H. L. Roediger, III and J. D. Karpicke,
"The Power of Testing Memory, Basic Research and
Implications for Educational Practice,"
Perspective on Psychological Science, 1 (2006), pp. 181–203

Many colleges fear that interference by parents prevents students from developing into independent adults. Parents, for example, are not allowed to see their college report cards. What is a parent to do?

—*New York Times*, July 30, 2006

What math and science teachers teach, what state standards expect and what states assessments test are, are rarely the same.

—A. C. Porter, "Teaching Standards, Test Found Not Aligned,"
Education Week, 2001

In a study done by one of our authors, in 1957, between modern disciplinarians and traditional [teachers], traditional teachers gave out less punishment in the classroom, used less sarcasm, were liked less and were thought to teach more, than their modern counterparts.

—Max Weiner, dissertation, *The Relationship of Concepts of School Discipline to Practice*, Yale University, 1957

National standards represent a real opportunity for public schools to turn themselves around and win back the confidence of the people that we serve. If we can agree on what we want students to learn, we can focus our energies, our ideas and resources on helping them achieve. Without standards we have no way to determine which reform ideas and programs really work.

—Albert Shanker, Governors/CEO's Education Summit, 1996

Any standard—rather than none—makes it easier to develop teacher training programs. Specialty training defines professional expertise.

—E. Rozcychi, "Establishing National Recognized Educational Standards," *Educational Horizons* (1997), p. 99

- There is no scientific data to support high-stakes testing.
- There is no evidence that any amount of homework improves the academic performance of elementary school students.
- At best, most homework studies show an association that is not a causal relationship.
- Homework studies and test scores confuse grades with learning.
- The results of national or international exams raise further doubts about homework's goals.
- There is no evidence that supports the idea that homework provides non-academic benefits.

—A. Kohn, "Abusing Research: The Study of Homework and Their Example," *Phi Delta Kappan* (2006), pp. 8–22

PART IV EVOLVING ISSUES

While single-sex classes have the potential to raise the achievement level of both boys and girls and to have a positive impact on the atmosphere . . . , these gains will be achieved only if the initiative is developed within gender-relational contexts.

—M. Younger and M. Warrington, "Would Harry and Hermione Have Done Better in Single-Sex Classes? A Review of Single-Sex Teaching in Coeducational Secondary Schools in the United Kingdom," *American Educational Research*, 43 (2006), pp. 579–620

Academic optimism made a significant contribution to student achievement after controlling for demographic variables and previous achievement.

—W. K. Kong, C. J. Tarter, and A. Woolfolk-Hoy, "Academic Optimism of Schools: A Force for Student Achievement." *American Education Research Journal*, 43 (2006), pp. 425–446

By the time they are four years old, children growing up in poor families have typically heard a total of 32 million fewer spoken words than those whose parents are professional.

—D. Kirp, "After the Bell Curve," *New York Times Magazine*, 2006, p. 16

In the following cities the percentage of public school teachers who send their children to private schools are:

L.A. — 18.9%
N.Y. — 21.4%
Boston — 24.4%
Miami — 35.4%

—J. Ricocco, "Just Facts—1998," *Education*, December 20, 2005

SUPPLEMENTARY READINGS

Adler, M. (1982). *The Paideia proposal*. New York: Macmillan.

American Heritage. (2003). *Roget's II: The new thesaurus*. Wilmington, MA: Houghton Mifflin.

Banks, J. (2007). *An introduction to multicultural education* (5th ed.). Boston: Allyn & Bacon.

Banks, J. (2006). *Cultural diversity and education*. Boston: Allyn & Bacon.

Barth, R. (1990). *Improving schools from within*. San Francisco: Jossey-Bass.

Benjamin, H. (1939). *The saber-toothed curriculum*. New York: McGraw-Hill.

Bennett, C. (2006). *Comprehensive multicultural education: Theory and practice*. Boston: Allyn & Bacon.

Bereiter, C., & Engelmann, S. (1966). *Teaching disadvantaged children in the pre-school*. Englewood, NJ: Prentice-Hall.

Bloom, A. (1987). *The closing of the American mind*. New York: Simon & Schuster.

Bowles, S., & Gintis, H. (1976). *Schooling in capitalist America*. New York: Basic Books.

Brown, C. (1965). *Manchild in the promised land*. New York: Signet.

Carter, S. L. (1991). *Reflections of an affirmative action baby*. New York: Basic Books.

Chubb, J., & Loveless, T. (2005). *Bridging the achievement gap*. Washington, DC: Brookings Institute Press.

Clark, K. (1965). *Dark ghetto*. New York: Harper & Row.

Coleman, J. S., et al. (1966). *Equality of education opportunity*. Washington, DC: U.S. Department of Health, Education and Welfare, Office of Education.

Coles, R. (1997). *The moral intelligence of children*. New York: Random House.

Conant, J. (1961). *Slums and suburbs*. New York: McGraw-Hill.

Counts, G. (1932). *Dare the schools build a new social order?* New York: John Day.

Covello, L. (1967). *The social background of the Italo-American child*. Leiden: E. J. Brill.

Cremin, L. (1990). *Popular education and its discontents*. New York: Harper & Row.

Cuban, L. (2003). *Why is it so hard to get good schools?* New York: Teachers College Press.

Darling-Hammond, L., & Bransford, J. (2005). *Preparing teachers for a changing world: What teachers should learn and be able to do*. Hoboken, NJ: Jossey-Bass.

Fantini, M. (1974). *Public schools of choice*. New York: Simon & Schuster.

Friedman, T. (2006). *The world is flat*. New York: Farrar, Straus & Giroux.

Gardner, H. (1997). *Extraordinary minds*. New York: Basic Books.

Gilligan, C. (1993). *In a different voice*. Cambridge, MA: Harvard University Press.

Glazer, N. (1997). *We are all multiculturalists now*. Cambridge, MA: Harvard University Press.

Glazer, N., & Moynihan, D. (1964). *Beyond the melting pot*. Cambridge, MA: MIT Press.

Goodlad, J., & Anderson, R. (1987). *The non-graded elementary school*. New York: Teachers College Press.

Greenawalt, K. (2005). *Does God belong in public schools?* Princeton, NJ: Princeton University Press.

Holt, J. (1967). *How children fail*. New York: Pitman.

Holt, J. (1967). *How children learn*. New York: Pitman.

Howell, W., & Peterson, P. (2005). *The education gap: Vouchers and urban schools*. Washington, DC: Brookings Institute Press.

Jensen, A. (1973). *Educability and group differences*. New York: Harper & Row.

Kounin, J. (1977). *Discipline and group management in classrooms*. New York: Holt, Rinehart & Winston.

Kozol, J. (1967). *Death at an early age*. Boston: Houghton Mifflin.

Kozol, J. (1991). *Savage inequalities: Children in America's schools*. New York: Crown.

Krantz, L. (2002). *Jobs rated almanac*. Fort Lee, NJ: Barricade Books.

Lazerson, M. (2004). *The education gospel: The economic power of schooling*. Cambridge, MA: Harvard University Press.

Leana, F. (1998). *The best private schools and how to get in*. Burlington, MA: Princeton Review.

Marcus, S., & Vairo, P. (2006). *Hot-button issues in education*. Lanham, MD: Rowman & Littlefield.

McCourt, F. (2005). *Teacher man*. New York: Scribner.

Merriam-Webster. (2003). *Merriam-Webster collegiate dictionary*. Springfield, MA: Merriam-Webster.

Ornstein, A., & Levine, D. (1981). *Teacher behavior research: Overview and outlook*. Bloomington, IN: Phi Delta Kappan.

Peterson, P. (2006). *Generational change: Closing the test score gap*. Lanham, MD: Rowman & Littlefield

Ravitch, D. (1983). *The troubled crusade: American education 1945–1980*. New York: Basic Books.

Ravitch, D. (2000). *Left back: A century of failed school reform*. New York: Simon & Schuster.

Ravitch, D. (2003). *The language police: How pressure groups restrict what students learn*. New York: Knopf.

Reis, R. A. (2001). *The everything hot careers book*. Avon, MA: Adams Media.

Schlechty, P. (2005). *Creating great schools: Six critical systems at the heart of educational innovation*. Hoboken, NJ: Jossey-Bass.

Sentiles, S. (2005). *Taught by America*. New York: Beacon.

Silberman, C. (1970). *Crisis in the classroom*. New York: Random House.

Simon, S. (2002). *Jackie Robinson and the integration of baseball*. Hoboken, NJ: Jossey-Bass.

Sowell, T. (1993). *Inside American education: The decline, the deception, the dogmas*. New York: Free Press.

Staples, B. (1994). *Parallel time: Growing up in black and white*. New York: Pantheon Books.

Steele, S. (1991). *The content of our character: A new vision of race in America*. New York: St. Martin's Press.

Sternberg, R. (1997). *Successful intelligence: How practical and creative intelligence can determine success in life*. New York: Plume.

Takaki, R. (1993). *A different mirror: A history of multicultural America*. Boston: Little, Brown.

Tienda, M., & Mitchell, F. (2006). *Multiple origins, uncertain destinies: Hispanics and the American future*. Washington, DC: National Academies Press.

Webber, T. (2004). *Flying over 96th street: Memoir of an east Harlem white boy*. New York: Simon & Schuster.

Wilson, W. (1988). *The truly disadvantaged: The inner city, the underclass and public policy*. Chicago: University of Chicago Press.